Growing Fruit
A Complete Guide to Growing Fruit at Home

Jason Johns

Copyright Information

Table of Contents

Introduction

One of the greatest pleasures for any gardener is growing their own fruit. Home grown fruit is delicious, full of flavour, and incredibly healthy for you! With governments across the world focusing on health, growing your own food makes a lot of sense because you have easy access to fresh fruit without the cost of buying it from the supermarket.

There is a huge amount of fruit you can grow at home, even if you live in a colder area and this book will tell you how to grow many different types of fruit at home. Even if you live in colder areas, you can grow some of the tropical fruits indoors if you want to. They will not grow to full size as you must grow them in containers, but they will still produce fruit.

For anyone who wants to grow their own fruit, this book has all the information that you need. Whether you want to grow apples, pears, strawberries, or more exotic fruits you will find growing guides and information here.

Having grown my own fruit for years I can attest to the fact it is so much nicer than anything you will buy in a store. My youngest daughter refuses to eat strawberries from the stores as they apparently "don't taste like strawberries" yet when strawberry season is upon us, she is out in my strawberry patch eating as many as she can! I've had to start growing my strawberries in vertical planters, so she can't reach them, and some can make it to the table.

You can freeze or can your fruit; make jams, jellies and other dishes; or store some fruits whole. Apples will last for months if stored properly, whereas some fresh fruits will only last for a few days even when stored in the refrigerator.

Fruits are incredibly versatile in what they can be used for and you will love growing them at home. It doesn't matter if you just have a small balcony or a large garden, you can still grow fruit at home. Nowadays, you can buy dwarf versions of most of the popular fruits and you can grow others in hanging baskets or even wall mounted planters. The new, columnar fruit trees take up almost no space at all, meaning they are ideal for anyone to grow, particularly people living in urban areas!

Growing your own fruit is something I would recommend to everyone and with this book you can get started growing your own fruit trees and bushes at home, reaping the many benefits of home-grown fruit.

Tips for Planting Fruit Trees

This section will give you some general guidance on how to plant various types of fruit plant so that they grow well and with as few problems as possible.

Fruit Trees

When you buy a fruit tree it will either come as a bare root plant or be already planted in a container. If you are planting your fruit trees in the ground then the soil needs to have good drainage and you should dig in plenty of rich, organic matter to give the tree a good head start in life.

If your fruit tree arrived as a bare root plant, then you are best to leave the roots soaking in a bucket of water for several hours or overnight before planting. This gives the tree a chance to revive itself before it is put in the ground and helps it get established. If you have bought your trees mail order, then this is vital as they will have gone without water for several days. Putting them directly into the ground makes it much harder for them to recover from being in the postal system.

If you do not have time to plant your bare root trees immediately, allow them to soak in water for up to 24 hours and then temporarily put them in the ground. This process is called 'heeling them in', and you plant them in a shallow hole at an angle, where you leave them for a few days until you are ready to plant them in their final location. It is not always possible to get your plants in the ground straight away, so this makes sure they survive long enough for you to plant them properly.

You can move fruit trees, but you need to make sure you take a big rootball with it and keep the roots damp and out of the sun while it is being moved. Be aware that once the tree has established itself, moving it could well prove fatal. Move trees while they are dormant, to prevent too much stress, and then look after them well. Young trees can easily be moved, but older trees are much harder to move because they have an established root system. I wouldn't recommend moving a tree older than four or five years without some major digging gear to remove a large rootball.

Take a note of where the graft is on your fruit tree and always make sure this is about 2" above the ground because otherwise the tree can revert to the type of tree the rootstock is.

Cane Fruits

These will always need a good, free-draining soil as they are deep rooting. They prefer a position in full sun but will tolerate partial shade, though may fruit slightly later. Remove weed roots and large stones from the soil and dig in organic matter before planting.

Cane fruits typically come as bare root plants though you can buy some types in pots. If they are bare root plants, then you need to soak the roots in a bucket of water for a few hours or overnight to give the plant a chance to revive itself. Do not leave a bare root plant out of the soil for any longer than you have to as the longer it is out of the soil, the harder it will be for it to come back to life! I have kept bare root plants in a bucket of water for a week before planting them out, but had I not they would probably not have survived.

Plant the canes in rows about four feet apart so there is room for you to get in between the rows and pick the fruit. A common problem people have with cane fruit is that they plant them too close, not realizing how much they can grow in a year. You are then left with the option of getting prickled picking your fruit or leaving it to rot on the cane!

You may see new canes shooting up out of the ground at the end of the first year with some fruits.

These are great and will bulk out your row a little, but you need to be careful you do not get overwhelmed by this new growth and your manageable rows turn into a nightmare fruit maze. I have autumn fruiting raspberries on my plot and they are forever putting up new shoots where I don't want them. While it is great for me to get new plants, they grow through my paths and other vegetable beds and are quite invasive. These types of fruit often benefit from being grown in containers.

Many fruit canes, particularly blackberry and its relatives, will benefit from being supported by wooden posts being put along the row and wire strung between the posts. Most raspberry cultivars do not need supporting, though some of the taller ones can. The canes are then tied to the wires to provide some support and prevent wind damage.

Bush Fruit

Bush fruit is relatively easy to grow though plants such as blueberries are fussy, needing ericaceous compost and watering with rain water only due to their need for an acidic soil.

The fruit from your strawberry plants needs to be kept off the ground to prevent rotting and pest damage, but the plants themselves are easy going.

Keep them mulched with straw and that will help keep the bugs off and your plants healthy.

Many of the bushy fruits will do very well in pots with strawberries doing well in planters. This allows you to grow fruit in a small space and have control over the soil which is important for the fussier bushes.

Common Fruit Problems

Growing most fruits will be trouble free. This section will detail some of the problems that are common across the different types of fruits and action you can take to make a healthy harvest.

Some of the most common problems faced when growing fruit are:

- Pests
- Diseases
- Poor drainage
- Late frost

The first two issues have been covered individually for each fruit, though ensuring your fruit plants aren't damaged, leaf debris is removed from the ground and regularly inspecting them for pests will minimize these issues.

Poor Drainage

Probably the biggest killer of fruit plants is poor drainage. Most trees do not like waterlogged soils and will object strongly if their roots get wet, often resulting in disease, a poor harvest or death. Planting your tree in a heavy clay soil is going to cause a lot of problems so you need to adjust the soil using grit, sand and organic matter so that the drainage it better.

You can test the drainage by digging a hole about 18" deep and filling it with water. If it takes more than three hours to drain, then your soil has poor drainage and needs amending.

Once you have amended the soil, you will be able to plant your fruit trees. However, depending on what you are growing it may be better to use raised beds where you have control over the soil conditions.

Late Frost

As a lot of fruit bushes and trees flower in early spring (April in many areas) there is still a danger of frost. If there is a frost, then it can damage the flowers on your plants which then means no fruit that year. Early fruiting varieties are at particular risk, so if you know you live in an area which regularly suffers from late frosts, look for a late flowering cultivar to grow.

Planting your fruit plants in a sheltered area where frost is less severe will help, but this is not always possible. Avoiding a south facing aspect will help the flowers to develop later, which means less chance of the frost killing them. However, some plants need to face south for the summer sun in order to grow properly.

 If there is a risk of frost, you can always cover your fruit bushes or trees with fleece to protect them from the frost. However, once the morning has warmed up, you will need to remove it to allow pollinators access to your flowers to do their job.

Late frosts are a pretty major problem as fruit plants rely on their flowers to produce a harvest. Once you see flowers on your fruit bushes or trees you need to start paying attention to the weather forecast and protect your plants when necessary.

Pests

Pests are a huge problem for fruit growers because they love fruit almost as much as you do and are incredibly destructive. It is soul destroying when your hard work is decimated by pests, but if you take care to remove leaf debris from around the base of your fruit plants and mulch the soil then it will help keep pests down. Ensuring there is sufficient air circulation around your plants and pruning well will go a long way to preventing many problems.

 As you have learned about each fruit you will have learned about some of the common pests and problems that affect that particular type of fruit plant, but some of the common pests you are going to encounter are:

- *Birds*: A real pest to fruit, so you need to net your trees or build fruit cages for your bushes. You can use bird scaring devices.
- *Aphids*: Another big problem for gardeners, but plant flowers to attract hoverflies, ladybirds and lacewings so they will eat the aphids. Planting nasturtiums at the edge of your garden as a sacrificial crop will also help to keep the aphid population under control. Make sure ants aren't farming the aphids and if they are, take steps to control the ant population as they will kill off the insects that prey on the aphids.
- *Apple Sawfly, Winter Moth and Codling Moth*: Keep the base of your plants clear of debris and remove and destroy infected fruit/leaves.
- *Deer, Rabbits and Squirrels*: These are very difficult to protect against and require fencing to keep them out and some good netting to protect the plants. If you are plagued by

rabbits, use a wire mesh fence that is dug two feet down into the ground to stop them burrowing under.

- *Raspberry Beetles and Big Bud Mite:* Hoe the base of your plants in the winter to dig up any pupae which are in the soil. Remove and destroy any infested plant material.
- *Red Spider Mite*: These can be deterred by regularly misting your fruit plants with water.
- *Slugs*: Frogs, toads and hedgehogs will eat slugs and snails so entice these friendly predators in to your garden. A small pond will attract toads and frogs, while hedgehogs can be attracted with canned dog food being left out. Beer traps and other deterrents can be used against slugs and snails, though their effectiveness is dubious and emptying a full beer trap is aromatic, to say the least! Going out at dusk or after a rainstorm and picking them off by hand and disposing of them is the best way to get rid of these destructive pests.

Disease

Disease can be a serious problem for your fruit crop if it is allowed to take hold. It can lead to a poor harvest or even the death of the fruit plant you have nurtured. Good hygiene around the base of your plant will help to keep disease down as will regularly checking your tree and pruning (and destroying) any infected leaves, fruit or branches. Do not compost any infected plant material, even if you are not sure if it is diseased. Remove it from your vegetable garden and destroy it to make sure that there is no chance of the disease spreading.

Regular pruning, good air circulation and feeding your plants regularly will help to reduce the incidences of disease. Make sure you buy healthy plants from a reputable nursery to ensure they are disease free. Should you live in an area that is prone to certain diseases, look for disease resistant varieties which will not be affected by the diseases. Stressed plants are more susceptible to infection, so regularly watering, feeding and maintaining will help your plants resist and fight of any diseases.

While you will not encounter these problems every day you do need to be aware of them. The earlier you can spot a problem and do something about it, then the more likely you are of being able to save the tree. Good hygiene and a good growing environment should be more than enough to keep your plants healthy and producing fruit for many years to come. Although we have put a lot of emphasis on diseases, you are not likely to encounter them very often. Pests are much more likely to be a problem for your plants.

Caring for Columnar Trees

Columnar trees are relatively easy to look after. Having been on the market now for over 30 years, these trees are bred specific to grow in a tall, single column, also known as vertical cordon fruit trees. The beauty of them is that you can plant the trees much closer together. This allows you to have a wider variety of fruit in a smaller space as columnar trees can be planted as close as 2-3 feet apart! So instead of having to settle for just one or two trees in your garden, you can grow a half dozen or more and have a wider variety of fruit.

Columnar fruit trees make for an excellent hedge or privacy screen. Planting them close together (40-50cm) in a row will create a great screen that also produces fruit. Alternatively, they can be kept in pots or planted around your garden as features.

Pruning Columnar Trees

Pruning these trees is generally very easy to do. In spring, cut back all side shoots of an apple tree that are longer than 20cm down to between 5-15cm. If there is a lot of growth, then do the same around the middle to end of June.

Pear trees are pruned in the same manner while cherry trees are pruned in the middle of summer after fruiting.

Generally, pruning is only performed to maintain the columnar shape.

Depending on the rootstock, some columnar trees can grow several metres high. Once your tree has reached your preferred height, cut the central leader (the main stem) to prevent it from growing upwards. Be aware that this can encourage more bushy growth from further down on the tree.

Planting Columnar Trees

While columnar trees will grow in containers, some people like to plant them in the ground. Before planting, rough up the rootball a little to tease out the roots. This will encourage the roots to grow outwards, which will provide better support for the tree and greater access to nutrients and water in the soil.

As a rule of thumb, the closer the grafting point is to the soil, the taller the tree grows. So if you do not want your columnar tree to grow too tall, make sure the grafting point is further out of the soil. The height of the grafting point can affect the growth of the tree by as much as 20%.

Ensure the hole is wide enough to accommodate the entire rootball without the roots being squashed up. Throw some slow release fertiliser or pelleted chicken manure into the bottom of the hole and then plant your tree as normal, firming down the soil around it.

Until it has established a strong root system, stake the tree to keep it stable.

Growing in Containers

Columnar trees will grow quite happily in pots, meaning they can be grown in an urban environment on a balcony or terrace. The size of the container will limit the size of the tree with most trees growing up to 150-180cm tall in containers.

Ensure the container has sufficient drainage holes in it. If not, then the pot will become waterlogged which can kill the tree. Fill the bottom few inches of the pot with a drainage material such as coarse gravel or Styrofoam. This helps to stop the roots from sitting in water, which can damage the tree.

Trees do better in pots that are not black simply because black pots heat up more in winter, which can then trick the tree into thinking that spring has come.

Use a good quality potting soil in the container and regularly feed your trees during the growing season. Remember that because the plants are in containers they are completely dependent on you for their food and water. Use a good quality fertiliser that has plenty of micronutrients in such as a seaweed based feed as this will help to keep the plants healthy.

Plant your trees to the same depth they were in the container they arrived in and then water in well. Move to a sunny but sheltered location and they will soon establish themselves and settle in.

Container grown plants should be moved in winter to a shady, sheltered location out of direct sunlight. If the temperature is going to drop below -5C, then wrap the container and the lower part of the stem with some insulating material such as bubble wrap and horticultural fleece. This will stop the cold from damaging the roots.

Thinning Out Fruit

Apple trees benefit from having the fruit thinned out to allow the tree to focus its energy on producing some great apples rather than lots of mediocre quality apples. You will generally see a fruit fall sometime in June where the tree naturally sheds some fruit.

After this, thin all fruit clusters to just one of two fruits. This allows the tree to develop good quality apples and ensures it does not weaken itself and become susceptible to diseases.

Cherries do not need thinning at all whereas pears benefit from thinning, but not to the same degree as apples.

Remember to feed and water your trees, making sure they don't become too waterlogged and prune them as normal. They will grow into healthy trees and produce fruit for many years, even when grown in containers.

Apples

Apples, *Malus domestica*, are probably the most widely cultivated fruit tree, with literally hundreds of varieties, even though you see maybe only half a dozen in the supermarkets. Many of the more unusual varieties are even more delicious than those found in the stores and are well worth growing. Most store-bought varieties are chosen purely because they store and transport well, with taste being a secondary concern. Apple trees are easily grown at home, will grow in most climates and are generally fairly easy to take care of.

At a Glance Facts

Planting Time:	Late summer/early autumn
Flowering Time:	Spring
Harvest Time:	Late summer/early autumn
Pruning Time:	Winter, when dormant
Hardiness:	Fully hardy
Height/Spread:	Varies on the cultivar and growing method
Aspect:	Varies depending on cultivar

Apples are deciduous trees and can grow anywhere between 15 and 40 feet (5 and 12 meters) tall, though there are dwarf and patio varieties available now that are even smaller. Largest varieties can be trained in fans, stepover or espaliers, which helps keep the trees manageable. The trees flower in spring with white flowers, often with a hint of pink and the fruit matures in mid to late autumn, depending on the variety. Apples can be eaten raw, cooked, juiced or made in to a cider, which makes them one of the most versatile fruits there is.

There are over 7,500 known varieties of apples with the world's largest collection to be found at the National Fruit Collection at Brogdale Farm in Kent, England.

There are three types of edible apples; dessert, cooking and cider though there are also crab apples which can be used for jelly but are otherwise not suitable for eating. Crab apples are high in pectin, which makes them a useful addition when making jams and jellies. Ornamental varieties of apple exist with smaller fruits, though these have no culinary use at all and should not be eaten. You can find eating apples in the wild; they grow easily from seed and where people throw apple cores out of a car window you can often find trees sprouting up in hedgerows and at the road side. There is a stretch of road near where I live that is notorious for its traffic jams. Down either side of the road are lots of pear and apple trees, all of which have grown from discarded fruit cores over the years.

Some of the popular varieties of English dessert apple, which have the best taste, are:

- Worcester Pearmain: This is a very sweet apple that smells like strawberries!
- Lord Lambourne: A classic dessert apple that is very juicy and slightly more acidic than other apples.
- Egremont Russet: One of the best apples with a dry texture but a very distinctive nutty taste. These can occasionally be found in the larger supermarkets in late autumn and should be snapped up when found! This is by far my favourite apple, and yes, I grow them because they are hard to find and expensive to buy.

Some of the most popular cooking apple varieties (these will taste sharp so should not be eaten raw) are:

- Bramley's Seedling: This has a very tangy and sharp flavour, producing large fruits that are greeny-yellow, often having some light red striping on it. This variety is often sold in supermarkets labelled as cooking apples.

- Cathead: This is one of the older varieties and produces very large round apples with a greenish-yellow skin.
- Allington Pippin: This conical shaped apple has greenish-yellow skin with a reddish flush and cream coloured flesh.

 There are many more varieties available, and you should look through a few tree catalogues and visit local suppliers to see what is available. Apples, like all trees, are a long-term investment, so you should always take care to buy something you are going to use and enjoy.

Apples are typically propagated by grafting cuttings on to the root of a new tree as growing from seed can produce brand new varieties and takes much longer to fruit. The label will tell you the rootstock, so you know how big the adult tree will grow.

You can grow apple trees in the ground, in pots or as espaliers along walls or a trellis, depending on the space you have available. Apples are not usually self-fertile, so you will need at least two trees to see any fruit. If there are other apple trees in the area where you live, then it isn't so important that you have multiple trees as they will be pollinated from these other trees. However, if you are unsure if there are other trees nearby, then buy your trees in pairs to ensure good pollination.

Apples are very early to bloom and there are not that many other plants in flower at the same time, so planting rosemary and primroses nearby will encourage bees to come and pollinate your apple trees. Different apple varieties flower at different times in spring, so if you are buying more than one apple tree, make sure there is some cross over in their blooming times to ensure that they will be pollinated. All of this will be indicated on the label.

There are some self-fertile varieties such as Jonagold which are useful if you do not have a lot of space.

 One of the main problems people face with apples is a late frost which kills off the flowers, stopping them from turning in to fruit. Apples like being planted on a slope or against a wall which will help to prevent frost damage. There are later flowering varieties such as Court Plendu Plat which can avoid

the worst frosts. Alternatively, fleece the tree before the frost hits to protect the delicate flowers.

If you do get caught out by a frost, then spray your apple tree with very cold water before the sun hits the flowers which will help the flowers adjust to the warmer temperatures.

Choosing an Apple Tree

Before you buy an apple tree you need to determine what height and spread of tree you want. The label will tell you how big the tree is going to grow. There are dwarf and patio varieties which will happily grow in containers and not take over your garden. Most larger varieties can be planted in large pots and will grow as big as the pot allows them to grow before their growth stops. With these trees, though, you need to monitor their health and prune regularly as when they become pot bound they can, occasionally, suffer from issues.

Apple trees are typically sold either as one-year-old or two-year-old plants. To get fruit sooner you are best buying the older trees. You can buy apple trees in most garden stores, though the selection is limited to the most popular cultivars. For more variety, look online or visit a specialist nursery.

Planting Your Apple Tree

Dig a hole that is deep enough to cover the soil mark on the trunk of your tree and wide enough so that the roots can spread out.

Part fill the hole with compost and put the roots in the ground. Place a stake in the ground at an angle rather than straight up as this helps support the tree and prevent movement or damage from the wind. Tie the tree to the support then fill the hole with soil and gently firm down. Careful not to tie the tree too tight to the stake and, ideally, use something that can be loosened as the tree grows to prevent damage to the trunk and bark.

Water the tree well and keep watered in dry spells. Within a couple of years, you should see some apples! Keep an eye on the tie on the stake and loosen it as required so it doesn't cut into the bark on the trunk. After a couple of years, when the tree is established, you can get rid of the support.

Harvesting Apples

Apples are ready mid to late autumn and you need to get them before they start to fall. Once they have fallen they cannot be stored and need to be used straight away, though you can cook and freeze them.

To pick an apple, hold it in your hand and give it a slight twist. If it is ripe then it will pretty much fall off in to your hand without having to force it. Be careful when harvesting your apples and ensure that you do not bruise them as this will cause them to rot, which then means they cannot be stored. Any damaged fruit can be used immediately, with the damage cut out and discarded.

Storing Apples

Apples need to be stored in cool conditions (36F / 3C) in a dark, well ventilated room, ideally one that is slightly humid. In reality, most people store their apples in a garage or shed. You can, of course, cook and freeze them or use any of a variety of preservation methods such as canning, bottling or making them into jam.

Apples can be stored in boxes filled with a layer of sand or you can get apple boxes from some supermarkets. You need to make sure that the apples do not touch each other when stored as that can cause them to rot. Some people use shelves like wine racks with the apples placed on the shelves instead of bottles. This works well because apples need the air to circulate around them to keep them fresh.

Common Pests and Diseases

Apple trees suffer from a number of different problems, with aphids being one of the most common, particularly on new growth. The usual treatments apply for aphids.

Codling Moths: These lay their eggs on the flowers and the larva develops inside the apple, eating its way out later in the year. Hang pheromone traps on the tree when it blossoms, which tell, you if there is a problem and then you can spray your tree.

Apple Scab: The leaves develop dark blotches and the fruit will have scabs on it. There are some trees which have resistance bred into them, but you can use sprays to prevent it.

Fire Blight: This is a bacterial disease which turns the leaves brown and then black as if burnt by fire. Prune the infected area back and clean your tools with alcohol afterwards. Make sure you use a sealant on the pruned areas to stop any infection entering the tree.

Apple Sawfly: This leaves ribbon like scars on the fruits from the maggots the sawfly leaves in the apple. The maggot burrows to the middle of the apple and causes it to drop, usually sometime in

July. There are sprays available to treat this problem or you can remove and destroy the infected fruits.

Pruning a New Apple Tree

Apple trees are pruned when young to shape them. This method works for both apple and pear trees that are one or two year's old which are being trained into a standard apple tree rather than a fan or espalier. It should be done between November and March while the tree is dormant. Taking the time to prune the trees early on can help to avoid problems later in life as they establish a productive, balanced branch system from the start. It works best on taller trees of at least five feet, usually on a more vigorous rootstock such as MM111 or M25.

When you are buying your apple tree, and the same applies for any tree, make sure it has a good, established root system and a sturdy stem. Always buy from a reputable source as you know the trees will be disease and pest free. Check the tree is healthy and alive, which can be tricky on dormant trees. The best way is to scratch the trunk or a branch close to the trunk slightly with a fingernail. Under the bark it should be green, which indicates it is alive. If it is brown, then it means the tree is dead.

One-year old trees are referred to as "maidens" and are sold as feathered or unfeathered. A feathered maiden tree has side shoots from the main stem and the ideal tree will be well-balanced with a goblet shaped branch system. An unfeathered maiden tree does not have side shoots, only having a single stem. These are cheaper than feathered trees, though be aware that some cultivars do not form feathered maidens.

Pruning should always be done when the tree is dormant, sometime between when the leaves fall and when the buds open. This is usually between November and the start of March. Always use a sharp, clean pair of secateurs when pruning and always make your cuts just above a bud and sloping away from it.

In the first year, a feathered maiden should have the central stem cut back to just above a strong, wide-angled shoot at about 2½ feet up the trunk. Make sure there are three or four shoots below this, evenly spaced out. On a dwarf tree, cut the central stem back to about 2 feet. Then shorten the shoots by between half and two thirds, making the cut just above an outward facing bud. Then remove any remaining lower branches.

In the first year, do not allow the tree to produce any fruit; remove it all as it forms. In the second year, providing the tree is growing well and has established itself, allow a couple of fruits to develop. From the third year, you can allow the fruit to develop as normal.

Apricots

 Apricots, *Prunus armeniaca*, are a surprisingly easy tree to grow that produces fruit prolifically and, with some new varieties, will grow well in cooler climates! These are a very unusual fruit to grow and one that will become a favourite in your garden.

At a Glance Facts

Planting Time:	November to March
Flowering Time:	Late winter to early spring
Harvest Time:	Mid July to early August
Pruning Time:	Early spring for young trees, summer for established trees
Hardiness:	Fully hardy but flowers are susceptible to frost damage
Height/Spread:	9-16 feet/3-5m depending on rootstock
Aspect:	Full sun or facing west

Apricot trees grow fast, and most are winter hardy, reaching a height of around 10 feet (3 meters) when fully grown. You can let them grow as normal trees, but it is better to train them to grow as a shorter bush, so you can reach the fruit. Just cut back the main stem when it reaches a height of five or six feet to encourage the tree to bush out. Remember to remove any branches that are growing vertically or rubbing together to keep the shape and height. Be careful about over pruning apricot trees as they can get infected through the wounds. Pruning should only be done in late winter or early spring while the tree is dormant.

When planting your tree, you need to leave enough room for it to grow into a bush; it can grow as wide as five feet! An alternative is to train the tree on a trellis in a fan shape, which is good for smaller gardens. The downside of this is that it needs more work, which increases the risk of disease, and you get less fruit, but it does mean you can grow apricot trees in smaller gardens.

Bare root trees can be planted from October or November onwards, so they are in the ground by spring. Apricot trees like a free draining soil that has a lot of organic matter in it. It tolerates a chalky soil but will struggle in a heavy clay soil. The roots of an apricot tree like to spread out so they are not really suited to pots or areas where they have to compete for space.

Apricot trees are typically grown on rootstocks, so you need to keep an eye out for suckers coming up below the graft. If you see any of these, then remove them as close to the main trunk as you can immediately. They will develop in to the original tree and can impact the growth you want from your tree.

Apricots are grafted on to rootstock to limit their size, but as of yet there are no dwarf rootstocks available. Growing an apricot as a fan requires space on a wall of 11-16 feet wide and between six and eight feet high.

Some of the commonly available rootstocks are:

- Torinel – a semi-dwarfing rootstock with good tolerance of poor soil conditions. Grows to 10-11 feet/3-3.5m high
- Krymsk 86 – a semi-vigorous rootstock that tolerates heavier, wet soils. Grows to 11-13 feet/3.5-4m high
- St Julian – a semi-vigorous rootstock that is commonly used and tolerates many different soil conditions. Grows to 15-16 feet/4.5-5m high

A three-year-old tree can be expected to produce 20 to 30 fruits which will appear in clusters on wood that is at least a year old. Don't be tempted to thin out the fruits when you see them like you would with other trees.

As the season progresses, the fruit will begin to swell, which is when you need to start watering the tree regularly and well. Once the fruits are ripe they will come off the tree very easily. Under or irregular watering can cause fruit drop, so keep an eye on how much water your tree is getting.

Although you need to prune your apricot tree, you need to avoid pruning in wet weather or bad winters as this will increase the chances of your tree getting a disease. If the winter is particularly wet or cold, wait until the start of spring when it is slightly warmer to prune it. Make sure the area around the base of the tree is kept free from weeds and debris, which will help give your tree more nutrients as well as protecting against disease and pests.

Fan shaped trees need fleece to protect them from late frosts, though when they are grown as bushes they do not need this extra help. However, in very cold areas, they can benefit from some protection during the coldest months.

Common Pests and Diseases

Apricot trees are susceptible to several different pests and diseases, but by buying a good quality, certified root stock plus looking after your tree and its environment, you can minimize the risk.

Mealy Plum Aphid: This small, soft bodied, green coloured insect is covered in a white mealy wax and in higher levels of infestation can cause stunted growth and black soot mould. The eggs overwinter, then hatch in the spring. Use Neem oil to control the population or other appropriate insecticides.

Peach Twig Borer Larvae: This brown and white insect with a black head feeds on the fruit and causes the shoot tips to die back. The larvae overwinters in rough areas of bark on older wood. Treating your apricot tree with insecticide when the flowers open should rid your tree of this pest.

Rust: This causes pale yellowish green spots on both sides of the leaves which will turn bright yellow. The fungus overwinters in leaves that remain on the tree or in twigs. Prevent by spraying with an appropriate fungicide every month for three months before the harvest in areas which are prone to the disease or later in areas where the disease appears later on.

Verticillium Wilt: This withers the leaves on branches that are a year or so old, making the leaves dull and stunted. It also affects the fruit, with older trees unable to recover from this disease. The fungus lives in the soil or plant debris. Keeping the plants well fertilized and watered helps to keep this disease at bay.

Shot Hole Disease: This causes brown lesions with purple edges on the buds, twigs and fruit and, in later stages, there will be holes in the leaves. The buds turn brown or black and start to exude sap. This can be combated by applying Bordeaux mixture before the autumn to protect the plant over winter.

Powdery Mildew: This causes powdery white patches of fungus on the leaves and fruit which may turn a leathery brown colour and crack. Applying an appropriate fungicide during flowering and fruiting keeps this disease at bay.

Brown Rot Blossom: This kills off the young blossoms as well as the leaves and twigs they grow on. You can find small tan coloured cankers on the twigs and spore masses on the flowers. This fungus overwinters in old fruit and dead twigs, so clearing fallen debris can help protect your plant. You can spray with an appropriate fungicide which will protect the plant, particularly during heavy rainfall.

Harvesting & Storing Apricots

Apricots are best harvested when they are ripe, rather than picking them before they are fully ripe. Most cultivars will ripen over a three to four-week period, so you have a bit of time to use them.

Ripe apricots change from green to a yellow colour with a hint of orange. When ripe they are firm to touch but slightly soft too. The exact colour of the ripe apricot will depend on the cultivar but be aware that they soften and become over ripe very quickly. When over ripe, they bruise very easily and do not store well because they rot.

When picking the ripe apricots, be careful as you remove them, so you don't bruise the fruit. Put them carefully in to a container to transport them and do not stack them more than two or three deep, otherwise the bottom apricots will get bruised.

 Store your apricots in a cool, dry place and they will last for a week, sometimes up to three. Storing in a single layer will help reduce any bruising and help the apricots store longer. Apricots store best in a temperature of between 31-32F (-0.5-0C) with a relative humidity of 90-91%. Avoid storing them with any fruits that give of ethylene, such as bananas, as this will cause the apricots to ripen faster and rot.

Apricots are best processed before storing, whether you make jam, pies or can them. When made into something, they will store for much longer.

You can freeze fresh apricots too. Wash and half the fruit, removing the stone. Peel and slice or plunge into boiling water for 30 seconds if you are not peeling them (this prevents the skin getting tough when frozen). Cool the blanched apricots and either freeze directly, puree, or freeze in a sugar syrup. Pack in freezer bags, remove the air and seal them before putting in your freezer.

Recommended Varieties

There are many different varieties of apricot. Here are some of the most popular and commonly available.

- Tomcot – crops in mid-summer with large fruits with a crimson blush, reliable in cooler climates
- Moorpark AGM – a late variety producing orange/red fruits
- Flavorcot – a Canadian cultivar well known for being reliable and frost tolerant. The fruits are orange/red, juice and ripe by late summer
- Aprigold – a dwarf cultivar reaching around five feet after ten years' growth. Great for growing in containers, this produces a good crop of tasty, orange/gold fruits
- Alfred – a traditional variety, requiring good soil and a sheltered yet sunny site to produce its medium-sized, orange fruits

Blackberries & Raspberries

These two berries are some of the easiest fruits to grow in almost any climate. They are extremely forgiving fruits and require very little attention to produce huge masses of fruits every year! They are relatively pest and disease free with the main problem being birds, but netting your fruit keeps them off.

Blackberries (*Rubus fruticosus*)

Blackberries grow virtually anywhere and in any conditions. They are a common hedgerow plant, though you can buy thornless cultivated varieties which are less hazardous to pick and grow larger, sweeter fruits. If you are growing them at home, then I highly recommend the thornless varieties as they produce much larger crops, grow better and are so much easier to pick. The wild varieties tend to produce small fruits that are not as sweet as the cultivated varieties.

Blackberries prefer a sunny site with lots of organic matter; though remove any perennial weeds that will compete for resources. Plant in early spring around 5 feet apart. Prune the plants down to about 7", mulch with straw or compost and water well. Each year prune back the growth that produced fruit that year and mulch with animal manure. Blackberries produce fruit on the previous year's growth, so remove canes that have produced fruit every autumn. Tie them to a good support to keep the fruit off the ground and you should get an abundant crop.

At a Glance Facts

Planting Time:	Winter
Flowering Time:	Spring
Harvest Time:	Summer to autumn
Pruning Time:	Autumn
Hardiness:	Hardy
Height/Spread:	Varies according to cultivar
Aspect:	Sun or light shade

Raspberries (*Rubus idaeus*)

Raspberries are typically bought as one-year old canes and there are two varieties; summer and autumn fruiting. It is worth getting some of both as you will get fresh raspberries for much longer but be aware that autumn fruiting raspberries grow from shoots under the ground and are extremely prolific. They will grow everywhere in your garden and you will forever be pulling them, up from all over the place. The autumn variety is better in pots so that you can contain them and stop them from taking over your garden. Even in pots they will still send out runners through the holes in the bottom of the containers, so remove those every year.

At a Glance Facts

Planting Time:	November to March
Flowering Time:	Spring to summer
Harvest Time:	Summer to autumn
Pruning Time:	February for autumn fruiting, late summer for summer fruiting
Hardiness:	Fully hardy
Height/Spread:	Varies according to cultivar
Aspect:	Sun or part shade

Raspberry canes need to be planted around 3 feet apart and cut down close to ground level. Water them well and then when they start to grow give them firm support and tie them securely. Prune them back every year to encourage a good crop.

Occasionally raspberry leaves can turn yellow which indicates the plant is lacking in iron. Water it with a sequestered iron solution and it will return to full health. By feeding your raspberries every year you can avoid this, but you may encounter it during the growing season if your plants are in pots.

There are many different cultivars of both raspberries and blackberries, so look around to find one that is suitable for your area. A favourite raspberry variety is any of the golden raspberries. These are very unusual and very tasty!

There are many other varieties of these berries such as loganberries, tayberries and a multitude of other cross breeds. A. These varieties are worth growing, with many producing large, tasty fruits.

When growing berries, it is best to use organic feeds because chemical fertilizers can affect the taste and nutritional quality. Pelleted chicken manure or seaweed feed is good during the growing season and then mulch with an acidic dressing such as leaf mould, sawdust or bark.

Berries need protecting from birds, which means netting them. Whether you build a permanent fruit cage or a temporary one is up to you and depends on your growing area. Fallen fruit will attract wasps so should be removed as soon as possible.

Autumn fruiting raspberries are pruned back to ground level in spring. Summer fruiting varieties have the canes that produced fruit cut back to ground level late in the summer.

As the fruit ripens you can start to pick it and freeze them by putting them on a baking tray to freeze individually or putting them in to portion sized bags. Of course, you can eat them raw or use them straight away in dishes.

Common Pests and Diseases

Blackberries, raspberries and most of their derivative plants suffer from many of the common problems and pests faced by other fruiting plants including powdery mildew, leafrollers, borers and more. Generally, taking care to ensure the ground is kept free of debris and the plant is well fed and looked after will keep your plants healthy. As with many diseases, they will take hold if the plant is stressed or damaged so be careful pruning and check the plant regularly when watering and harvesting.

Buying quality canes that are certified disease free is a good way to ensure that you avoid many of the problems that can come with these fruits. Lack of air circulation is a frequent cause of fungal infections, which comes down to good pruning and spacing of plants. Tying the plants to fences will help to control them and give them the space they need.

Harvesting and Storing

Blackberries ripen slowly and are best picked over several days when they are fully ripe. These will store for a few days in your refrigerator. For long term storage they should be frozen or processed in some way. When harvesting, do not layer them too deep in a bowl as the bottom fruits will be squashed. Before freezing, wash the blackberries and then lay them on a cookie tray to put into the freezer. This freezes them individually. Once frozen, you can transfer them to freezer bags for long term storage.

Raspberries are one of those fruits that suddenly go from not ripe to over ripe, often overnight. Be very careful picking these as they are very easy to damage. Store in a single layer if you can when picking to prevent damage. Aim to pick them when they are firm and slightly squishy. Over ripe raspberries can still be used, but they are not good for storing unless processed immediately in some way. Freeze raspberries or process them in some way for long term storage, otherwise keep them in your refrigerator where they will last for a few days.

Recommended Varieties

The popular varieties of early season blackberry include:

- Black Butte – early season, thorny, producing large, long black berries with a good flavour that improves during cooking
- Lock Tay – thornless, semi-upright canes with compact growth making them good for smaller

gardens. Good flavour fruit and plant has good resistance to weather damage and fruits early in the season

- Sylvan – thorny, vigorous with good tolerance to wind, drought and heavy soils. Produces large, long fruit early in the season
- Waldo – thornless, good for smaller gardens with large, tasty fruit. Prone to viruses but is resistant to leaf and cane spot
- Loch Ness – thornless, good for smaller gardens, producing large fruit with a good flavour when ripe in mid-season
- Ouachita – mostly thornless, vigorous, producing large yields of good sized berries in the middle of the season
- Asterina – thornless, very vigorous, producing high yields of large berries with a good taste late in the season
- Chester – thornless, very vigorous, with a heavy crop of mid-sized berries with reasonable flavour late in the season. Best grown in sheltered areas in the north, but has good disease resistance

Some popular autumn fruiting raspberry varieties include:

- All Gold – produces sweet, yellow fruit from mid-August to mid-October. Growing to around 6 feet high, this cultivar has good disease resistance

- Autumn Bliss – grows to around 5 feet high and happy to grow without support. High disease resistance, including aphids, and produces delicious fruit from August to late October
- Joan J – a thornless variety that produces a good yield even in its first year. Good disease resistance with a high yield in August which drops off until around October

Some of the most popular summer fruiting raspberry varieties include:

- Tulameen – popular with commercial growers because it stores well and produces a heavy crop. Has good disease resistance and grows up to 6 feet tall. Crops between mid-Jul to mid-August
- Glen Magna – bruises very easily, so not suitable for commercial crops, but has a delicious flavour and is ideal for the home grower
- Malling Admiral – produces deep red, large fruits and has good disease resistance. Requires support as it produces large canes that are susceptible to wind damage
- Ruby Beauty – a dwarf variety, growing to just 3 feet tall, so ideal for containers

Blueberries

 Blueberries, *Vaccinium corymbosum*, are a miracle super food, packed full of vitamins and nutrients that are very good for you. Experts say you should be eating these regularly for the anti-oxidants and the other health benefits they provide to you.

At a Glance Facts

Planting Time:	November to March
Flowering Time:	Spring
Harvest Time:	Mid-summer to early fall
Pruning Time:	Winter
Hardiness:	Frost hardy to fully hardy
Height/Spread:	18"-7 feet/45cm-2m
Aspect:	Sunny and sheltered

Growing Blueberries

Blueberries prefer a well-drained, acidic soil that has plenty of organic matter in it. The ideal pH of the soil for a blueberry is 4.0 to 5.2 and it may be worth testing the acidity of your soil before planting these berries to ensure it is suitable. If the soil has a pH above 5.0 then the plant can develop an iron deficiency, which will impact its ability to produce fruit and could kill the plant. You can get around this by regularly feeding your plant with sequestered iron, but an acidic soil is best.

One trick gardener's use with blueberries is to plant them in a pot with some old iron nails in the bottom, which ensures the plant gets enough iron. However, you can just feed the plant with a sequestered iron liquid feed.

Blueberries can grow into large bushes up to seven to ten feet high and grow well in pots as they are so fussy about the soil. Always make sure you water them with rain water, as water from taps can contain lime, which affects the soil pH level.

These plants like full sun or partial shade, though you will need at least two blueberry plants, so they can cross fertilize and produce a larger crop of fruit.

 Plant these berry bushes at any time of the year in pots or in the autumn or spring straight in to the ground. Prepare the soil first with plenty of organic matter and either sawdust or chipped bark as these will make the soil more acidic.

If your new bush has flower buds or new growth you can remove these when you plant it out so that it focuses its energy on developing a strong root system.

Blueberry bushes need spacing around 4 to 5 feet apart and in holes that are 1½ feet deep and wide. Always keep your blueberry bushes well-watered and do not let them dry out. If you do not have rain water to hand, then mix vinegar with tap water to make slightly acidic water the plant prefers.

For the first two or three years you, only need to prune blueberries if there are any damaged or diseased branches. After this, though, you need to give your plants a prune every March to cut back the older wood which does not produce fruit. It is easy to prune, just remove any old, dead or spindly looking branches plus any that look like they will touch the ground when they bear fruit or cross over and touch. Cut the twiggy wood at the end of a branch away by cutting back to the first upward pointing branch or bud

The older wood is grey in colour and it can be cut back either to ground level or to the first young looking side shoot. Blueberries can send out suckers which pop up nearby which should also be removed to prevent the bush from spreading itself too thin.

You can find that a blueberry bush will produce an abundance of fruit one year and then none the following year. This is common, and you will need to prune the bush back the following spring to encourage less but more regular fruit production.

Common Pests and Diseases

There are a few problems which affect blueberry plants but provided there is enough air circulation, full sun, and the ground is kept free of debris you should avoid most of the problems people encounter.

By far the biggest problem will be birds. They love blueberries almost as much as you do, and you will have to net your bushes several weeks before the berries ripen. Net your plants or use other bird deterrents but be aware your crop will vanish quickly if you do not protect it. The birds will eat your crop before they are ripe, so don't leave it too late to cover them.

There are a few insects that bother blueberries, namely cherry fruit worm, plum curculio, blueberry tip borer and cranberry fruit worm. Keep an eye on your plants and if you see any problems in the fruit or leaves then you will have to use an appropriate pesticide. In most cases you are not going to see these pests.

Blueberries can be affected by some fungal diseases such as leaf spot and powdery mildew, though there are resistant varieties. Replace the mulch around the bottom of your plants every year and this will prevent fungal spores overwintering there. If you need to use a fungicide, then ensure it is one that is safe to use on edible plants.

Canker: This is one disease which can affect blueberries and you will notice small reddish spots on the canes which grow larger and eventually kill the cane. If you spot this, you need to prune out the affected wood to a good foot below the canker.

Mummy Berry: This is one of the more serious fungal infections and the first indications of it are flower clusters that blacken. The fruit will turn a tan colour, become hard and look like they have been mummified. Remove any infected areas of the plant and destroy them.

Chlorosis: The leaves of the plant will start to turn yellow which is usually a sign of iron deficiency in most plants. Typically, with a blueberry, it means the pH of the soil is too high and it needs to be adjusted. Test your soil with a pH testing kit and adjust the quality of the soil appropriately.

Recommended Varieties

There are five main types of blueberry grown in America:

- Lowbush
- Northern Highbush
- Southern Highbush
- Rabbiteye

- Half-High

The most common variety is the northern highbush, which tends to have a good level of disease resistance. Highbush cultivars are self-fertile; though cross pollination will allow them to produce larger fruits. Neither rabbiteye and lowbush are self-fertile, both needing a plant of the same type to produce fruit.

In the UK, there are a number of cultivars available, all of which are cold hardy and many of which are dwarf plants. Some popular varieties include:

- Earliblue – an early ripening cultivar that produces large, light blue berries with a good, sweet flavour
- Bluetta – a compact variety that spreads rather than grows upwards and produces a medium sized berry
- Patriot – produces very tasty, large blue berries. This vigorous, hardy cultivar is known for producing large yields
- Herbert – considered by many to be the tastiest blueberry
- Bluejay – a mid-season berry that produces a reasonable yield of medium to large berries with a good but slightly tart flavour
- Coville – a late variety that produces large fruit which will remain on the tree for a long time

Cherries

Cherries, *Prunus avium*, belong to the same family as plums, apricots, peaches and almonds and there are numerous varieties growing all over the world ranging from ornamental to edible.

There are two types of edible cherry plants; sweet and sour. The former is the best for eating while the latter is used in cooking and jam making. The two varieties do not cross pollinate so if you want to grow both you will need two plants of each type. The Morello sweet cherry is self-fertile, so you only need one tree.

Cherries are expensive to buy in the stores because they have a very short fruiting season and are difficult to pick, store and transport. Growing them at home gives you access to delicious fresh cherries in July or early August, though you may struggle to beat the birds to them if you do not net your tree early enough. Birds love cherries and will empty a tree overnight, being happy to eat them before they are ripe.

At a Glance Facts

Planting Time:	November to March
Flowering Time:	Mid-spring
Harvest Time:	Summer
Pruning Time:	Young trees in spring, established trees in early to mid-summer
Hardiness:	Fully hardy, but susceptible to frost damage to flowers
Height/Spread:	10-26 feet/3-8m by 5-13 feet/1.5-4m depending on rootstock used
Aspect:	Full sun, ideally south or southwest facing

Cherry trees can grow up to 10m tall, though there are some dwarf and patio varieties available now. If you get a standard cherry tree, then you may want to prune the main stem into a bush shape or train it along a trellis, so you can pick the fruits easily. They are a very hardy tree and will even be happy trained to grow against a north facing wall!

The trunk of a cherry tree is usually a reddish brown colour with the blossom appearing first, following by the leaves. Cherry blossom is renowned for its beauty and is considered a sign that spring is here. In Japan, ornamental cherry trees are planted purely for their blossom and the cherry flower is highly prized.

Cherry trees like a nice light, well-drained soil such as a sandy loam. The fruits are quite delicate and can be damaged by rain or hail. A late frost after the flowers have appeared will cause them to drop, so you need to fleece the tree if there is any risk of frost.

Common Pests and Diseases

Like many of the other plants we have talked about, good sanitation, watering and air circulation will keep many pests and problems at bay.

Probably the biggest challenge you will face with a cherry tree is birds as they love cherries and will eat them before they are fully ripe. I remember moving into a house with a huge cherry tree in the garden. I was very excited to get cherries the next year, watched them grow and then woke up one morning to find the tree completely stripped of not quite ripe cherries! Cherry trees must be netted to keep the birds off and ensure you get any fruit from your tree. Do this several weeks before they are ripe to keep the birds away.

Aphids: These can be a major problem for cherry trees and can be combatted by planting wild flowers near your tree which will encourage predators such as ladybugs and hover flies. With the worst infestations you will need to use an organic, gentle spray or pick them off by hand.

Borers: These will bore small holes in the trunk and you can find leaves and branches wilting, turning brown and dying. Watering well will help to combat these pests as will regularly fertilising your tree. These are very difficult to control, and you can spray the trunk and larger branches if required, though do not spray smaller branches as it could kill the tree. If you do have borers, then you are best consulting a professional arborist for assistance.

Silver Leaf: This is a fungal disease and on some trees, you will see leaves taking on a silver lustre, though often the first sign is twigs and branches die back. This is a tough disease to treat and you can confirm the diagnosis by cutting a 1" diameter branch, wetting the cut surface and checking for a brown stain in the wood. Cut out the diseased areas and destroy the infected wood. Use a pruning sealant to cover any wounds over ½" in size. There is no chemical control available for this disease.

Powdery Mildew: Another potential disease that causes spots on the leaves that turn yellow and often causes leaf drop. You can see white patches on the underside of the leaves, which will be the fungal spores. Rake up and dispose of fallen leaves every fall as a preventative measure and spray with an appropriate fungicide.

Brown Rot: This affects small branches, flowers and fruit, causing them to rot and shrivel. You will see tufts of grey/brown spores on leaves, twigs or fruit. Prune and destroy any infected areas. There are fungicides that can be used to combat this but remove any fallen fruit and leaves to reduce the risk of infection.

Harvesting and Storing Cherries

 Cherries need to be stored in a refrigerator, in a perforated plastic bag, where they will remain usable for up to ten days. Do not wash them before storage as it encourages rotting but wash them before eating.

Cherries can also be frozen whole or halved and pitted. Spread them out on a baking tray not touching, freeze them and then bag them up when they are firm.

Commercially, cherries are harvested with a tree shaking machine. These are not really practical for the home grower, but you can still shake the tree. The downside of this is that many of the cherries will be bruised as they fall, even if you catch them in some netting.

Ripe cherries are firm and fully coloured. Sweet cherries are best tasted to ensure they are mature as the sugar content rises significantly just before they turn fully red. Sour cherries are ripe when they easily come off the stem. Be patient as cherries do not continue to ripen when removed from the tree.

If rain is forecast, remove the cherries quickly as the rain can cause them to split. In all likelihood, you will be picking cherries for a week to ten days as they all ripen. Remove the cherries by hand but be careful not to damage the woody spur they are attached to as they will produce fruit next year. If you are not planning on using the cherries immediately, leave the stem attached to the fruit. If you are planning on cooking or canning your harvest, then you can leave the stem on the tree and just remove the cherry.

Recommended Varieties

Here are some of the most popular sweet cherry varieties:

- Rainier Cherry – great for eating fresh with the ripe fruit being mainly yellow with a red blue. They have a great texture and are very sweet.

- Van Cherry – produces a medium sized fruit that is very firm and black when ripe. They are another very sweet cherry that is great to eat fresh, can or cook with.
- Bing Cherry – a large cherry that has a deep maroon colour when ripe. They are commonly found in supermarkets and have an excellent, sweet flavour. This variety has a particularly short shelf life, so needs using soon after picking.
- Santina Cherry – a sweet, black cherry that is oval shaped. Harvested in mid to late June, this cherry is great fresh or used to cook with.

Currants – Black, White & Red

There are three main types of currents we will discuss here, red, white and blackcurrants. These are popular in Europe, though rarer in the USA where grapes and blueberries are preferred. However, there are some good health benefits from currants; blackcurrants are extremely high in vitamin C and are meant to help with joint inflammation too!

Currants are very easy to grow, and do not take up a massive amount of space if they are well pruned and maintained. All three types of bushes have very similar growing requirements, though blackcurrants are the most popular due to their taste and use in cooking and cordials.

Redcurrants produce lovely red berries that have a tart flavour. Whitecurrants are translucent with a much more delicate flavour; many people say the flavour is so delicate that they don't taste of anything, making these the least popular currant. Blackcurrants are just sweet and loved by children across Europe for their juice! Blackcurrant juice isn't as popular in the USA, with grape juice being drunk instead.

Redcurrants (*Ribes rubrum*) / Whitecurrants (*Ribes rubrum* 'White Grape')

 The different colours of the berries make for a very pretty addition to your garden plus the leaves are a blue/green colour too. These plants can be grown as bushes or trained to grow in a fan shape or cordon. They are easy going plants that are not high maintenance and so long as they are pruned correctly, will produce a good crop of fruit every year.

At a Glance Facts

Planting Time:	October to March
Flowering Time:	Spring
Harvest Time:	Summer
Pruning Time:	Spring to early summer
Hardiness:	Fully hardy
Height/Spread:	2-6 feet/60cm-1.8m
Aspect:	Sunny, but tolerates light shade

The plants prefer partial shade as strong sunlight can damage the leaves. They enjoy a well-drained, moist heavy soil and so do well in clay soils though less well in sandier soils. However, if you are growing them in clay, then dig in lots of organic matter to improve drainage.

Both red and white currants produce fruit on old wood. In winter, remove any diseased or very old branches. At the start of summer, cut back the new growth to two buds which will keep the plants compact. Prune leaders to outward facing buds, unless the branches are bending towards the ground in which case you should prune to an upward facing bud.

In early spring, established cordons are pruned by cutting the new growth on the main stem to a quarter of the growth from the previous year. If the branches are weak, cut by a half. To keep the growth straight, cut to a bud that is on the opposite side to last year's cut. When your cordon is at the height you want, cut to a single bud of new growth every year as spring ends.

These types of currants grow well in pots, though they are susceptible to root rot in winter. Raise the containers up on feet or bricks, which will allow the drainage holes in the pot to do their job.

Container grown currants need feeding every two weeks from late winter through to early spring. As with many other pot grown plants, every year before summer, remove the top couple of inches of soil from the container and replace with fresh compost. It is recommended to repot these currants every three years. Either transplant to a bigger container or remove a third of the compost and roots and return to its original pot.

Blackcurrants (*Ribes nigrum*)

 Blackcurrants like similar conditions to their red and white cousins, though they are more tolerant of waterlogged soils. To get a good crop of berries you will need to feed the blackcurrants regularly throughout the growing season.

At a Glance Facts

Planting Time:	October to March
Flowering Time:	Spring
Harvest Time:	Summer
Pruning Time:	Late autumn to winter
Hardiness:	Fully hardy
Height/Spread:	5-6½ feet/1.5-2m
Aspect:	Sunny, but tolerates light shade

You can buy ready grown blackcurrant bushes, or you can grow them from cuttings cut to 9" to 10" in length. Just push three quarters of the cutting into the soil in a pot, firm down around the cutting and water. Leave it outside over winter and come spring it should come to life!

When you plant a blackcurrant, dig a large hole so the roots can spread out and dig some compost in to the bottom. Water the hole well then put the bush in the ground, ensuring it is upright before you return the soil. Firm down the soil around the plant and keep it well watered for the first few months while it establishes itself. It will also appreciate the water during the growing season to allow the blackcurrants to swell up. You will get a small crop of berries in the first year of planting a bought blackcurrant, though it will take several years for the plant to reach maturity and give a good yield. Saying that, in the second year after planting my blackcurrants, I got a good pound of fruit from each bush.

In autumn they will benefit from a prune and a mulch of well-rotted animal manure to give them the nutrients they need over winter.

Blackcurrants are pruned while dormant, from late autumn through to late winter. The best fruit is produced on younger wood, so you are aiming to remove the older wood, leaving the newer branches behind. For the first four years, try to keep a basic structure of between six and ten strong shoots, removing any weak shoots. In the fourth year, cut about a third of the older wood away at the base to encourage younger shoots to form. Remove any weak shoots and any that are leaning down to the ground.

The berries will ripen from mid-summer and you can harvest the berries by snapping or cutting off the truss holding the berries and then removing them in the kitchen. You can pick them individually, but it is more time consuming and you are more likely to damage the berries. The berries do not ripen all at the same time and if you leave them, they can become over ripe and split. The berries can be stripped from the truss using a kitchen fork, though be careful not to damage any berries.

Common Pests and Diseases

As with most soft fruit there are a few pests and diseases with the most prominent being birds. They love currants and will happily strip your bushes for you and do it quickly and efficiently! While scarecrows and other deterrents are moderately effective, the only true way to protect your currants is with a fruit cage or netting.

Aphids: Although these are unlikely to kill your plants they are going to seriously impact fruit development. You will find them initially on the tender tips of the plants and they will soon spread. Pick them off and destroy them the first time you see them or use an organic spray. Blackcurrants are particularly susceptible to aphids on the new growth.

Big Bud Mite: In January and February when the buds are forming they will grow much larger than normal. They will either fall off or produce distorted growth which does not produce fruit. This is incurable, and you can leave the plant to grow, removing any fallen leaf debris quickly, harvest the fruit and remove the bush and destroy it. There are varieties such as Ben Hope which have some resistance to this.

Reversion Disease: This commonly follows an infestation of big bud mite and cannot be treated. Any affected plants need digging up and destroying immediately. The flowers will be malformed and after three years your bush will stop producing fruit, with the fruit production declining every year. The Ben Gairn variety has some resistance and can be planted to replace infected bushes.

Mildew: This greyish powder is unlikely to kill your plants but will significantly impact fruit production. Pruning and spraying are your only treatments, though the Titania and Ben varieties have some resistance. Remove all touching or crossing branches so they can't rub and introduce infection.

Run-Off: If you notice the fruits falling off your plants before they are ready, then you likely have this problem. It can be caused by poor watering or by cold weather. It can occur one year and then the next year your plants are fine. You need to determine the cause and take the appropriate action or grow resistant varieties such as Ben Sarek.

Wilting Leaves: This is commonly caused by vine weevils damaging the roots, unless your plant has been seriously under watered. You will have to dig around the roots and check then use an appropriate spray or nematodes to get rid of the pest.

Woolly Scale Insect: These leave white patches on your bushes, usually on the weaker parts of the plant. They can occur if you are late pruning. These bugs are difficult to kill with sprays and your best bet is to put on a pair of gloves and remove the bugs from the white patches and squish them by hand. You can use a toothbrush to get rid of the white patches, just make sure you catch the bugs themselves.

Harvesting and Storing

Harvest currants in the summer when the fruits are juicy and firm. Cut the whole truss of fruit off and either store in your refrigerator for a few days or use straight away. The fruit trusses can be put into plastic bags and frozen.

Popular Varieties

Some popular redcurrant varieties include:

- Jonkheer van Tets – produces an early, very heavy crop of large berries
- Red Lake – a heavy cropper that is disease resistant
- Rovada – great in containers with good disease resistance
- Stanza – a late flowering variety, ideal for cooler areas with late frosts

Some popular whitecurrant varieties include:

- White Imperial – widely available, produces lots of small, low acid berries
- White Dutch – early ripening with sweet, juicy berries

Some popular blackcurrant varieties include:

- Ben Hope – produces heavy yields and is resistant to leaf spot, gall midge and mildew
- Ben Lomond – a late flowerer, producing heavy yields of berries ready in late summer
- Ben Sarek – a compact plant, growing no more than 4 feet high, this is ideal for containers or smaller gardens. Producing large berries, it has resistance to both frost and mildew

Figs

 Figs, *Ficus carica*, were originally grown in Asia, though were adopted by the Mediterranean people and soon became a staple food for them. Coming from such a warm climate you would be forgiven if you thought they were something that couldn't be grown in a colder climate like the United Kingdom, America or other countries at similar latitude. However, they grow very well outdoors in those areas.

At a Glance Facts

Planting Time:	Spring or autumn
Flowering Time:	Early to mid-Spring
Harvest Time:	Late summer to early autumn
Pruning Time:	Varies depending on growing method
Hardiness:	Hardy, but embryonic fruit requires protection during extreme cold
Height/Spread:	10-13 feet/3-4m
Aspect:	South or west facing, sheltered

Figs are unusual and are not eaten very often by countries other than those on the Mediterranean.

They are a fun tree to grow and their large leaves make for an interesting addition to any garden. Grow them against a good south facing wall and you can expect one crop each year though under glass you can grow more varieties and usually get two crops of figs each year.

Fig trees are best grown in a fan shape with their roots restricted by using a large pot or a two-foot square brick box going down two feet in the soil. There is no need for a bottom to this box, just fill the last six inches with gravel so the roots spread out. If left to its own devices planted in the ground then the tree will often just produce leaves and few, if any fruit.

Fig trees like to be well watered and when the fruit is starting to form you need to feed it with a high potash fertilizer such as a tomato feed. It benefits from weekly feeds and pruning even two or three years to encourage new growth.

When winter comes you need to remove any fruits that haven't ripened otherwise they can end up damaging the tree when they rot. Leave the small embryonic fruit on the tree as in warmer areas, these will form into a second harvest. Woodlice are attracted to the fruit and will damage them if you do not remove them and red spider mites are a pest attracted to fig trees. This latter pest can be removed by hosing the tree with water every few days.

Birds love figs, as do wasps, so you either need to net the tree or put bags round each fruit to protect them so that they can ripen fully.

While a fig tree is frost hardy, new growth can be killed off by the cold over winter, so it is worth protecting the tree with fleece or straw.

There are plenty of varieties of fig trees out there and *Ficus Carica* (Brown Turkey) is a popular one as you do not need to restrict the roots, though it produces fewer fruits than White Marseilles which produces a later crop but likes being kept in pots.

Unlike many other fruits, figs do not ripen when they have been picked. Ripe figs will start to split their skin and, if they have a slightly sour smell, then they have gone past their best.

Figs need to be handled carefully as they are easily damaged. Fresh figs will store in a refrigerator for two or three days at most, though are best picked and used straight away. If you do store them in your refrigerator, then leave them to come up to room temperature before eating them.

Figs are very sweet and are a great accompaniment to goats' cheese or prosciutto, or eaten raw with honey or clotted cream!

Fig trees need pruning to maintain their shape and health. With bush and half standard trees, you are aiming for an open crown and balanced tree so that light gets into the centre. You will need to prune three times a year:

- Early Spring – remove branches that are crossed, damaged to do not adhere to the shape plus cut away any suckers from the ground. Cut back any branches that have become too long
- Early Summer – pinch out the new growth at six leaves, but do not prune from July onwards
- Autumn – remove large figs that haven't ripened but leave the embryonic fruit in place

Larger trees that have been neglected can end up becoming very leggy and will not produce a lot of fruit. In early spring, prune off the older, bare branches of your established tree, leaving a 2" stub if you want more growth from that point. If you have to remove more than a quarter of the branches, avoid doing it all or once, but spread the work out over two or three years, performing it in February each time.

Many gardeners like to grow something a little bit different and a fig tree is well worth growing – it is an interesting tree to grow, does not need a large amount of space and produces a fruit that is hard to find and expensive to buy.

Common Pests and Diseases

Keeping an eye on your fig trees and checking them when you water them will help you stop pests or diseases getting a foothold on your tree and causing damage. Here are some of the common problems that affect fig trees and how to deal with them.

Fig Rust: This causes the leaves to turn a yellow/brown colour and fall off towards the end of summer. A closer look at the leaves will show rust coloured spots on the bottom of them. This is not usually fatal, but it will weaken your plant and affect the crop. Neem oil has been shown to help if you catch the infection early, but keep the base of the fig tree clear of debris to help stop the rust.

Leaf Blight: This is another fungal affection which attacks the leaves, causing yellow spots that appear to be water soaked. Over time these will spread and dry out, leaving a papery like surface behind and thin holes will tear in the leaf or it will die. The best control is removing affected leaves immediately and keeping the ground around the plant clear of debris.

Pink Blight: A colourful yet irritating disease that can kill a fig tree if left unchecked. It produces a pink or white coloured velvet like coating on dead or dying branches which will spread rapidly. Cut out and destroy all diseased parts of the plant and thin the branches to allow good air circulation.

Fig Mosaic: This is a viral infection that starts off with yellow spots on the leaves which eventually develop into rust coloured bands and the fruit can drop, appear spotted or be stunted. Unfortunately, there is no cure for this particular disease and infected trees need to be removed and destroyed to prevent the spread of the virus.

Fruit Souring: This makes the figs themselves turn sour and can often be spotted by bubbles or ooze coming out of the fruits together with a fermenting smell. It is believed this is transported by insects, particularly vinegar flies or fruit beetles so careful insect control will prevent infection.

Root Knot Nematodes: These are very hard to spot, and their symptoms look very similar to other root diseases. If your tree is infected with these pests, then they will decline gradually and be less vigorous. In time, the roots will develop swollen galls which block the root system and cause the tree to due.

Unfortunately, these are almost impossible to get rid of because they hide in the roots.

Harvesting and Storing

As figs do not continue to ripen once picked, they are harvested when ripe and used within a few days. You cannot leave them on the tree as they will become too ripe and develop a sour taste. Figs are ripe when the fruit necks begin to wilt and the fruit hangs downwards. Pick your figs too early, and they will not have a pleasant taste. While the fruit is perpendicular to the stem, the fruit it not ripe and should not be picked. A ripe fig is soft to touch and gives off a nectar when fully ripe. The fruits ripen at different times, so you need to harvest them as and when they are ripe. It is better to pick a slightly overripe fig than one that is not quite ready.

Determining when a fig is ripe can be a bit tricky as the different varieties have different colours indicating they are ripe. The colours can vary from a green through to dark brown. However, you will soon learn when the figs on your tree are ripe. For the best results, harvest in the morning.

Ripe figs are very delicate and susceptible to bruising, so you need to be gentle when picking them and handing them. I recommend cutting the stem rather than pulling as there is less chance of damaging the fruit or knocking other ripe fruits from the tree. Leave some of the stem on the fruit when harvesting as this does help to delay spoilage.

Store the figs in a shallow dish and do not stack them as they will bruise. Be aware that the fig tree produces a milky white sap which can cause itchy dermatitis in some people which is made worse by sunlight. If you are allergic to latex, wear gloves and a long sleeve shirt, avoiding contact with this sap.

Figs should be eaten, dried or frozen as soon as possible after picking. Dried figs that are then frozen will last up to three years in your freezer. Figs will store in a refrigerator for around three days, though do not put them near any other vegetables as they will cause them to rot.

Popular Fig Varieties

You might be surprised to realize that there are over 700 fig tree varieties, though most of them are of no interest whatsoever to the home grower. Fig varieties fall into four types:

- Caprifigs – only produces male flowers, never produce fruit and only exist to pollinate female fig trees

- Smyrna – only produces female flowers and require a caprifig to pollinate it
- San Pedro – produces two crops, one on new wood that needs pollination from a male flower and one on older wood (usually leafless) but doesn't require pollination
- Common Figs – the type you are likely to grow at home that does not require any pollination

Some varieties of common fig that are good to grow at home include:

- Alma – produces fruit late in the season, but they do have an excellent flavour
- Brown Turkey – a popular variety for growing at home, producing large, delicious figs over a long growing season
- Celeste – a large tree that produces small to medium sized fruits that are brown or purple when mature. Produces good quality fruit that ripens early in the season
- Purple Genca – produces large, dark purple fruits with a lovely, sweet flesh

Gooseberries

Gooseberries are a delicious fruit that is ideal in crumbles and jams, but better still is full of thorns and makes for a handy yet productive hedge for any areas that you have security concerns about! We planted them along the back of our property to help discourage people wandering into our garden, and they were very effective, even keeping the neighbourhood cats out!

This plant is divided into two types. The European gooseberry, *Ribes grossularia*, which grows to about an inch long and the American gooseberry, *Ribes hirtellum*, which grows to about half an inch in length.

At a Glance Facts

Planting Time:	October to March
Flowering Time:	Spring
Harvest Time:	Summer
Pruning Time:	Spring to early summer
Hardiness:	Full hardy
Height/Spread:	2-6 feet/60cm-1.8m
Aspect:	Sunny, but tolerates light shade

Gooseberries do not need a lot of attention, though you need to prune out the middle each autumn to ensure the air flows around the plant properly. Sawfly love gooseberry leaves, unfortunately, and are one of the few pests you will find attacking this plant. These can be combated by putting rhubarb leaves on the ground under your gooseberries and removing the pests when you spot them.

Gooseberries are not a popular fruit, with them rarely being seen in shops. You can find them at pick your own farms or farmer markets, but due to their delicate nature and the difficulty picking them, they just do not work well for shops. Occasionally, they can be found in season in the more expensive shops though, typically, you will need to grow your own.

There are plenty of different varieties of gooseberry with the most commonly seen plants bearing green fruit, but red, white, black and yellow fruits exist and are equally delicious. The different varieties can be early or late fruiting, hairy or smooth or even sweet or sour! There is a huge variety and many of the sweet cultivars taste great raw or cooked!

Some of the most flavourful varieties are Green Gem and Invicta though Lord Derby is a popular red gooseberry and Leveller produces a very tasty yellow fruit. One of the best though is Victoria, but this is increasingly difficult to find.

Gooseberry bushes are popular with gardeners because you can pretty much leave them to it! They prefer a good well drained loam soil, though will do well in any type of soil. The plant is not too fussed how much sun it gets, though dessert gooseberry plants do prefer a sunny aspect.

Gooseberry plants like to be mulched once a year with a good quality compost or manure. This will help to ensure good growth the next year and a good crop of fruit.

 Come winter time you can prune the main growth shoots back by around half which will promote new growth. Any branches that are weak or do not bear fruit need to be removed. You want to produce a goblet shape to allow air flow around the fruit.

You can train gooseberries into fans or even single, double or triple cordons; they are a very versatile plant. Once you have one plant, you can take cuttings and grow new plants from them; it isn't difficult to do.

Gooseberries need to be washed, then top and tailed before use. Dessert varieties do not freeze well and should be kept in your fridge, unwashed, until you are ready to use them. Green cooking gooseberries will freeze very well.

Common Pests and Disease

Gooseberries, like other soft fruit, require protection from birds so you can net them or use something like strips of plastic to deter them. A fruit cage is an ideal solution but is not practical for everyone, so you may need to use fine mesh netting.

Aphids and caterpillars may attack your gooseberry plants, which can be dealt with using an insecticide or natural pesticide. If you can see the caterpillars, then you can pick them off by hand and crush them between your fingers or otherwise dispose of them.

Mildew is a problem that affects gooseberries, which is why you need to ensure there is sufficient airflow around the plant and between the branches. If you get mildew, then remove and destroy any fruit or leaves immediately.

Occasionally, you will see the edges of the leaves looking like they have been scorched. This is typically a potash deficiency and is remedied by carefully forking in about an ounce of sulphate of potash for each affected plant.

Harvesting and Storing

When you pick gooseberries depends a little on what you are going to use them for. If you are making preserves such as jam or jellies, then the fruit is best picked slightly unripe while they are still firm. If you are eating them or making pies, then pick the berries when they have softened and are fully ripe.

There are a lot of different gooseberry varieties and determining when they are ripe varies according to the cultivar. Some cultivars are green when ripe, some red, some have a blush of pink and more. The best way to determine if a gooseberry is ripe is to give it a quick squeeze. A ripe gooseberry will have a little give when you squeeze it.

Gooseberries do not ripen all at once, so you will be harvesting them for several weeks. It is a good idea to have multiple plants purely so you can pick a decent amount at one time to cook with.

It's best to pick gooseberries with care and thick gloves! The thorns are very sharp, and you are likely to get scratched no matter how careful you are. Pull the berries off the branch and put them in a bowl. Berries that have fallen to the ground are not worth saving as they are overripe. These should be removed and composted.

Pick a couple and taste them to ensure they are ripe enough for you.

 You can speed up the picking process by putting a sheet under each bush and shaking it, but many people feel this damages the fruit and plant. Continue to harvest gooseberries while they are on the bush until they are all ripe.

The berries are best used immediately or frozen for use later. They will store for a few days in your refrigerator. Any unripe berries can be turned into a preserve or canned.

Popular European Gooseberry Varieties

There are a lot of different gooseberry cultivars available, and which you buy will be determined by a number of factors, including:

- Are they early, mid or late season croppers?
- Can they be eaten raw, cooked or both?
- What colour are the ripe berries?
- What disease resistance does the plant have?

European gooseberries are larger than their American counterparts and can be any colour from white to yellow to red, purple and green. Here are some of the most commonly found varieties:

- Achilles – a mid-season variety producing a large, red fruit that is very sweet. Great for cooking when green or eating raw when ripe
- Early Sulfur – a yellow, fuzzy fruit that has a great flavour, but the plant has little disease resistance
- Greenfinch – produces pale, green berries mid-season with some resistance to mildew
- Hinnonmaki – a variety from Finland that has a tart skin and sweet flesh
- Invicta – a popular variety with good disease resistance. It produces large fruits, but they are somewhat bland when compared to other varieties
- Telegraph – produces large, yellow fruits that sadly don't have much flavour
- Tixia – a thornless hybrid with some disease resistance and producing red fruits
- Whinham's Industry – a thorny plant producing yellow fruit with a good flavour

Medlar

Medlars, *Mespilus germanica*, are a fruit which have, sadly, very much fallen out of favour, having been popular in medieval times in the United Kingdom. They are a very unusual fruit which has an interesting flavour and is commonly made in to jams or jellies. They are self-fertile, so you will need just a single tree and they are worth growing just because they are so unusual and rare!

At a Glance Facts

Planting Time:	Autumn
Flowering Time:	Late spring to early summer
Harvest Time:	Late October to early November
Pruning Time:	Winter
Hardiness:	Hardy
Height/Spread:	20-25 feet/6-8m
Aspect:	Full sun to light shade

Medlars are available mail order or occasionally from larger garden stores. They are most commonly used as ornamental plants today, but the fruits are well worth harvesting. Occasionally, you can find medlar trees in the wild or they can be found in stately homes and the grounds of other old buildings. Make sure you buy an edible version rather than one of the many ornamental versions.

This fruit prefers a well-drained, deep and fertile soil but is quite tolerant of most soil conditions except chalky or poorly drained soils. They can be grown in partial shade, but prefer a warm, sunny site with good shelter. The leaves and flowers can be damaged in high winds.

The trees grow to between 13 and 20 feet in spread and height and are usually grafted on to a rootstock, so keep your eyes out for suckers. The trees can be planted between November and March with about 15 feet between trees. For the first three or four years they will need staking to support them while they establish themselves.

 In March, provide the plant with a good feed and then mulch with a good compost or well-rotted manure. They will need regular watering, particularly in the first three to five years to ensure they establish themselves well.

Each winter the tree will benefit from a pruning to maintain a good shape and encourage it to produce plenty of flowers and fruits the following year. You can train them as espaliers and prune them in a similar manner to an apple tree.

Common Pests and Problems

Medlars are not bothered by many pests and diseases, though occasionally winter moth caterpillars will take up residence. These can be picked off by hand or sprayed with an appropriate spray. You may also find aphids on soft, new growth and these can be managed in the normal way.

Harvesting and Storing

Harvest the fruits in later October to early November just before they are fully ripe, though pick them before the first frosts hit. They are best harvested when it is dry and the ripe fruit will easily come off the tree.

Before eating a raw medlar you need to "blet" them, which is where you dip the stalks into a strong salt solution to preserve them and stop them from rotting. They can be stored in trays, so they are not touching with the eye facing downwards in a cool, dark and frost-free place. After two or three weeks the flesh will become soft and brown.

Recommended Varieties

There are several medlar varieties available, with the most popular and common being:

- *Mespilus germanica* 'Dutch' – produces a large fruit on a tree with a spreading habit
- *Mespilus germanica* 'Nottingham' AGM – a more upright tree, producing smaller fruits but with the best flavour
- *Mespilus germanica* 'Royal' – a fairly upright tree, produces a medium-sized fruit
- *Mespilus germanica* 'Large Russian' – produces a large fruit that has a good flavour

Pears

 Pears, *Pyrus communis*, like apples, are widely cultivated and the fruits can be eaten raw, used in cooking, juiced or turned in to alcoholic drinks! The pear tree is in the same plant family as the apple tree and the flowers look very similar.

At a Glance Facts

Planting Time:	Late autumn to early spring
Flowering Time:	Spring
Harvest Time:	Autumn
Pruning Time:	November to early March
Hardiness:	Hardy but susceptible to frost damaging the flowers
Height/Spread:	Depends on cultivar and rootstock
Aspect:	South or west facing

Pear trees can grow to over 50 feet in height and are normally a tall, narrow shaped tree. A few species are shrubby in nature and both dwarf and patio versions are available.

There are a lot of varieties of pear, though not as many as apple. Like apple though, only a small handful of the varieties are found in stores with many of the best tasting varieties not being grown commercially due to difficulties storing and transporting the fruit. There are two main types of pear, eating (dessert) and cooking, the names indicating what the pears are good for.

Two of the most common pear cultivars are Conference and Concorde, both of which are found in stores. These are relatively easy to grow, and trees of both varieties are easily found.

Pears can be grown in the ground or in pots plus you can sometimes find them growing in the wild from discarded fruits or where birds have spread the seeds. The similarities between pear and apple extend to cultivation, pollination and propagation.

You can grow pears from seed, though the more common way to grow them is with grafting a pear branch onto the rootstock of pear, apple or quince. This ensures the variety of pear is maintained while benefiting from the properties of the rootstock. Quince A rootstock is the most common and is great for bush or espalier trees. Quince C rootstock is a little less vigorous and is ideal for cordons but can be used for bush and espalier trees too.

Pears are a deep rooting tree and like a light, sandy soil. However, many varieties of pear are grown on quince tree rootstock and so are more shallowly rooted. The latter variety is also better suited for clay soils and large pots.

 You can grow pear trees just like apple trees, i.e. in pots, as trees or train them as espaliers. You will need two trees to ensure that they produce fruit and can pollinate each other.

You can buy pear trees that are a year old, which are best suited for training as espaliers or buy two or three-year-old trees which will produce fruit quicker when put in to the ground.

Pears need to be planted in the autumn with full sized trees being around 30 feet apart and dwarf trees being around 18 feet apart. They need a sunny location and ideally a good, rich, well-drained soil. Be aware that there are ornamental pear trees that do not produce edible fruit, so please check you are buying an edible cultivar.

Consider how large the adult tree will grow when you choose a pear tree, which is determined by the rootstock. The type of tree you choose will depend on where you plan to site it.

To plant your tree, dig a hole a little deeper and wider than the root ball and part fill it with good quality compost. Place the roots in the hole, tie the tree to a support and fill the hole with soil, firming it gently. Water well and keep watered in dry spells and you should have pears within two years. Prune the tree to maintain the size and shape that you require.

Common Pests and Diseases

Pears suffer from many of the same problems as apples and, like always, vigilance and early treatment is the best form of prevention. Remove fallen leaves or fruit and keep the base of the tree free from other debris. Prune any diseased or damaged branches as well as any touching branches to prevent the introduction of infection.

Aphids: These are common and can be found on new growth. Get rid of them using the usual methods.

Brown Rot: A fungal disease which causes brown rot to spread through the fruit. Usually worse in wet summers, you may also see white fungi pustules on the surface of the fruit. Remove and destroy rotten fruit as soon as you spot them.

Canker: You may see deformed areas of bark and these need to be cut out and sealed with a pruning sealant.

Caterpillars: These may be an issue so keep an eye out and remove any cocoons that you find.

Gall Midge: This is a tiny fly that will lay its eggs in the flower buds before they open and hatch into maggots that feed on the embryonic fruits which then turn black. In late May and June, you will see the young fruit dropping from the tree and the maggots crawling into the soil. In the spring, cultivate the soil around the tree which will expose pupating maggots to wildlife. If you see any infected fruit, remove it and destroy it before it drops. There are sprays you can use on smaller trees.

Pear Leaf Blister Mite: A common problem on the leaves of pear trees, it causes yellow or red blisters to form which eventually turn black. Although the damage looks unpleasant, it has no effect on your pear crop. The only control is to remove and destroy infected leaves.

Pear Rust: This appears as orange spots on the top surface of the leaf and brown growths on the underside. The spores from the pear tree are then blown on to juniper trees where other spores germinate and blow back on to pears. The spores can travel up to three miles in ideal weather conditions, so you can find your tree gets infected even if there are no juniper trees nearby. Pruning out the infections can help you control this problem though fungicides labelled for powdery mildew and pear scab can help control this problem.

Harvesting and Storing

Pears must be picked before they are fully ripe as when ripened on the tree, they ripen from the inside out. By the time they seem ripe, they have gone beyond ripe and are mushy on the inside.

Harvest your pears when they are mature, but not fully ripe. A mature pear is still firm to the touch and the colour could be anything from green to yellow with a red blush, depending on the cultivar.

The easiest way to tell if a pear is ripe it to take the fruit on the tree in your hand and tilt it so it is horizontal. If the fruit is mature, it will come away from the tree when you do this, otherwise it is immature and will not come off.

Store your pears at room temperature for about a week and they will ripen sufficiently for eating. You can ripen them faster by putting them in a paper bag or with a banana, which gives off ethylene gas. Later fruiting pear varieties can require longer to ripen than early fruiting cultivars.

Recommended Varieties

There are many varieties of pear, with these being the most common and popular:

- Conference AGM – very popular dessert pear that produces distinctive, elongated fruits. It is a reliable and heavy cropper.
- Onward AGM – delicious and juicy, this is a reliable cropper, but the fruits do not store well and need eating quickly.
- Concorde AGM – a compact dessert pear that produces large yields

Persimmon

The persimmon, *Diospyros kaki*, also known as the Sharon Fruit is a very commonly grown "exotic" fruit and is widely prized due to its Latin name, *Diospyros*, which means food of the gods. It is a brilliant orange coloured fruit with an intense flavour and great texture.

At a Glance Facts

Planting Time:	November to March
Flowering Time:	Late spring
Harvest Time:	Late summer to autumn
Pruning Time:	Later winter to early spring
Hardiness:	Hardy down to 14F/-10C, depending on cultivar
Height/Spread:	Grows up to 40 feet high and 25 feet wide, depending on cultivar
Aspect:	Full sun, south or west facing

The tree is a good-looking tree, though slow growing. It will reach 15 to 20 feet tall and has dark green leaves that turn the most beautiful reds and oranges come autumn. With a heavy load of fruit, the branches will weep and need supporting as the leaves drop and the brightly coloured fruit is left in all its glory on bare branches.

There are two types of persimmon trees, Asian and American, with the Asian trees being less hardy, preferring the temperature to stay above 0F. The American version is hardier, withstanding temperatures as low as -20F. American persimmons are about the size of a plum while Asian varieties grow to the size of a peach. The American varieties grow wild across the northern half of the USA.

Asian persimmons can be astringent or non-astringent while American varieties are only astringent. Astringent persimmons make your mouth pucker and should only be eaten when they turn soft and mushy, i.e. fully ripe. The non-astringent varieties can be eaten while hard or soft. However, both varieties can be used in cooking.

Plant a persimmon tree in autumn or early spring in well-drained, slightly acidic soil. The plants benefit from full sun and need to be between 20 and 25 feet from each other. The American variety will tolerate more shade and soil variation than their Asian counterparts. The roots grow slowly, and the tree will appreciate regular watering throughout the season and when your tree hits 3 to 5 years old you should start to see fruit.

Be careful when fertilizing these trees, because too much nitrogen will cause the fruit to drop. Add 5 to 10 pounds of compost to the soil each winter though and the trees will be content.

 Typically, these trees are not self-fertile though the Meader variety (an American persimmon) is. American versions will not pollinate with Asian versions, so you will need two plants of the same type to ensure they are properly pollinated and produce a good crop of fruit. You will, ideally, need a male pollinator tree for your female trees to ensure you get fruit.

Trees are pruned and shaped in winter and you remove any suckers, which are more common in the American varieties. You may want to shape the tree when it is young so that you have a central leader system with between six and eight widely spaced scaffold branches around the trunk to support the fruit. Once the trees reach maturity and bear fruit, little pruning is required.

Persimmons can be harvested between September and December depending on what variety you are growing. The Asian varieties will need cutters to remove from the branches. The non-astringent varieties need harvesting while firm and with a full colour while the astringent Asian varieties can be harvested when the skin of the fruit becomes translucent. An American persimmon will fall from the tree when it is ripe.

Common Pests and Diseases

Very little affects a persimmon tree, making it ideal for your garden. Your biggest problem may be birds, who are rather partial to this fruit. Pick the fruit early and ripen them in a plastic bag with bananas for around a week in a warm room and the ethylene gas from the bananas will ripen your persimmons.

Harvesting and Storing

Astringent persimmon varieties should be allowed to fully ripen and soften on the tree. Just be aware that leaving them there too long allows your wild competitors chance to help themselves to your crop. This competition is most fierce during early autumn. You can net and protect trees grown at home, but this is not feasible for wild trees.

Typically, most people harvest astringent persimmon while they are still hard and leave them at room temperature to ripen. If you can protect your fruit from animals, then you can leave them on the tree until fully ripe. Harvesting an astringent persimmon is easy as they will come off the tree when ripe. If you are harvesting before they are fully ripe, use a pair of sharp scissors or hand pruners to cut the fruit free, leaving a small stem on the fruit. Do not stack your persimmon, particularly if they are fully ripe, as they will bruise very easily.

Non-astringent persimmons are ready to pick when they have their full colour and can be eaten straight away. You can leave them to soften, which does help their taste, but you do not need to leave them.

There is a myth that persimmon require a frost before they are edible which is false. Frost will damage unripe fruit and make them inedible.

Hard astringent persimmons will store in your refrigerator for a month, and often more, and can be frozen for around 8 or 9 months. Non-astringent persimmons do not store very well. They can be stored for a few days at room temperature but storing them in the refrigerator causes them to soften.

One of the best ways to store persimmon is to turn the fruit into a pulp and then freeze the pulp. This can be used for cooking, smoothies and so on.

Recommended Varieties

There are a few different varieties of persimmon that you can buy. Depending on where you live, you may find some of the American persimmon trees growing wild.

- Prok – An American persimmon that is quite hardy. An astringent variety that is self-pollinating, producing fruit that is great for baking.
- Yates – Similar quality to the previous cultivar.
- Fuyu – A non-astringent variety, self-pollinating tree growing up to 20 feet tall. The fruit is firm when ripe and deliciously crunchy, ideal for slicing.
- Hachiya – Relatively hardy, this self-pollinating tree grows up to 20 feet tall. The astringent fruit can be eaten raw or used in baking

Plums, Damsons and Gages

 Plums, *Prunus domestica*, are a popular fruit and come in a variety of colours from purple to blue to yellow and to the green of greengages (which are rare but delicious). They are often made in to jam, wine, and sauce or eaten as a fruit or dried to become a prune.

At a Glance Facts

Planting Time:	November to March
Flowering Time:	Early to mid-spring
Harvest Time:	August/September
Pruning Time:	Established trees are pruned in summer; young trees are pruned early spring after bud burst
Hardiness:	Fully hardy, but frost can damage flowers and affect fruiting
Height/Spread:	10-26 feet (3-8m) depending on rootstock
Aspect:	Full sun, south to west facing

The trees flower in early spring and are covered in blossom, giving cherry a run for its money. Typically, around half the flowers turn in to fruit, though this is influenced by the weather. A late frost can kill the flowers and too little or too much rain can also negatively influence the crop. In colder areas, planting late flowering varieties such as Oullins Gage, Blue Tit or Marjorie's Seedling can help avoid this problem.

Despite being a temperamental plant, they are popular to grow at home. There are a wide variety of different types of plums though I can very strongly recommend the greengage, *Prunus domestica subsp. Italica,* as they are amazing, though a lot of people prefer the darker purple and sweeter plums.

Plum trees will grow well in pretty much any climate; they like sun and produce a heavy crop of delicious plums around August to September time. Be aware that fallen fruit must be removed because it does attract wasps.

Plum trees come in a variety of sizes based on the root stock and can grow anything up to around 25 feet tall with a good spread. For the larger trees you are going to either need to be good at climbing trees (which is how we got them as kids in my parent's garden) or use a ladder, which we did when we were older. Most people though prefer the convenience of the smaller varieties or will fan train their plum tree.

You can grow a plum tree in a container and it will limit the growth of the tree to a smaller size. There are patio versions of plum trees available.

Sadly, plums don't get eaten as often as they should because people consider them to be a "messy" fruit. Like peaches, they are juicy, and the juice can drip out while you are eating it which puts some people off.

The fruit is available in many supermarkets though typically you will see one or maybe two varieties and that is it. There are hundreds of different varieties of plum tree and if you are growing them at home then varieties such as Czar are recommended which produce a yellow/green plum or the Old English Greengage which produces very juicy green fruit. Blue Tit is a blue plum that is very prolific and there are a wide variety of other plum trees that you can grow. It is much better growing these more unusual versions than the varieties grown in the store because remember, store bought fruits are not selected for taste but for ease of transporting and storage!

Home grown plums are delicious and I remember the tree in my mom's garden fondly. Every summer as children we would be climbing the tree gathering the plums and some would even make their way in to the house, with many being eaten in the tree. With such a huge crop of plums we were constantly giving them away to visitors and always made sure that mid-August we arranged for people to come visit so they could leave with a bag of plums!

 In the summer as the fruits are swelling, avoid any drought stress by regularly watering and mulching your plum trees. In late winter, the trees benefit from an application of sulphate of potash and a good, general purpose fertilizer. In early spring, a good layer of mulch helps keep the roots warm and protects the tree from water loss.

Not all plum trees are self-fertile, so you are going to need to check the variety you buy and buy more than one tree if they are not self-fertile.

Common Pests and Problems

Plums suffer from their fair share of problems but taking the usual precautions will help to minimize the risk of disease and pests attacking your fruit.

Plum Tree Leaf Spot: This is a bacterial leaf spot which attacks the leaves but is often unnoticed as it attacks the underside of them. In more advanced infestations you will see red ringed holes in the leaves. Planting resistant varieties of plums will help as will pruning away diseased branches.

Plum Sawfly: This shows as damage on the inside of the plum, though from the outside you may notice a small brown mark on the skin or a hard drop or two of resin on the fruits. Unfortunately, it makes the plum inedible. The sawfly lays its eggs in the blossoms of your tree in the spring and then these develop in to caterpillars which eat in to the plum as it develops. A pheromone trap can work in controlling these pests as can chemical sprays when the blossom first falls. In late February you can turn the top 3-4" of soil under the tree which will bring the sawfly to the surface where birds will eat them. Remove and destroy any infected fruit.

Aphids: Another common problem, indicated by the young leaves curling up. Pick off the aphids by hand or spray your tree. Encourage ladybirds and other predators into your garden which will dine on the aphids. Ensure ants are not farming the aphids and take steps to control the ants if they are.

Plum Moth: You will find pink maggots inside your plums, rendering them inedible; often, and most disturbingly, these are usually found when you bite in to a plum! You will see a small pink maggot and brown stuff (its excrement) inside the plum. On the outside, you may see a small entry hole together with some dried drops of gum. Chemical sprays will help, though obviously this can render your crop inedible. Pheromone traps also help, though the Victoria and Czar varieties of plum seem more vulnerable to plum moth.

Pigeons and Other Birds: They all love your plums and will wreck your tree and decimate your crop. Pigeons are not light and will break branches with their weight trying to get to the plums. Netting your trees will help as will building a fruit cage around smaller trees. Other bird scaring methods can help. Don't think you can distract the birds with bird food elsewhere in your garden, they will simple eat that and then move on to your plum tree!

Harvesting and Storing

Plums are very easy to pick from a tree and will come away from the branch easily when ripe. When they have fallen, the plums are typically overripe and are not so good for eating but can be used for cooking. Sometimes, after strong winds, you may find plums that are good for eating on the floor, but they will need using quickly as they will bruise and rot from their fall.

The fruit are ripe when they are slightly soft when squeezed. The plums need harvesting regularly as they do not all ripen at once and can very quickly become overripe.

Eat your plums fresh from the tree, make them into preserves or destone them and freeze them.

Recommended Varieties

There are many different plum cultivars available. Here are some of the most popular and commonly found trees.

Dessert Plums

These are plums that are suitable for eating but can also be cooked and turned into preserves or sauces.

- Blue Tit – a self-fertile, blue plum that grows well in more northern areas providing they are in a sunny, sheltered location. The fruit are ready to harvest around the middle of August.
- Victoria – a self-fertile, orange/red plum that is hardy and tolerates light shade. Harvest from late August through to early September.

- Opal – a self-fertile, orange/red plum that is a heavy cropper. It tolerates light shade but needs sun to develop the full flavour of the fruit. It is suitable for northern areas and the fruit is ripe early in August.

Gages

These produce round to oval fruit that usually have pale green flesh. The skin colour can range from green to yellow and some cultivars will have a blue or purple tinge.

- Cambridge Gage – a partly self-fertile cultivar that is very reliable. It prefers full sun, producing a good crop of fruit from late August to early September
- Imperial Gage – a self-fertile variety that is a reliable cropper. It has good disease resistance and the fruit ripen late August.
- Oullins Gage – a reliable, self-fertile cultivar that is good in northern areas. The fruit ripens mid-August.

Damson

Damsons are small, dark purple fruits that are similar to plums with a unique flavour. They are often found growing in the wild. Damsons are not good for eating raw, but great for making jellies, jams and even pies!

- Farleigh Damson – a self-fertile, hardy cultivar that is suitable for wet and northern areas. The fruit ripens around the middle of September.
- Prune – a self-fertile variety that tolerates partial shade and damp climates. It is a reliable cropper and suitable for northern areas. The fruit ripen early in September.
- Mirabelle - These are bright red to golden yellow, round, cherry sized fruits that are either eaten raw or used in cooking.
- Mirabelle de Nancy – a part self-fertile cultivar that is popular in France. The fruit are small and sweet, most often used for cooking or preserves. The fruit is ripe in August or early September.

Rhubarb

Technically rhubarb, *Rheum rhabarbarum*, is a herb though it is considered a fruit due to its sweet stems. It is a versatile plant that is popular in the UK where it is stewed and eaten with cereal or yogurt or made in to a crumble with apples or other fruit.

At a Glance Facts

Planting Time:	Flowering Time:
Flowering Time:	Early spring to late summer
Harvest Time:	Spring to summer, depending on cultivar, earlier if forced
Pruning Time:	November to March
Hardiness:	Full hardy, mulch well in winter to protect crowns
Height/Spread:	6 feet/2m across, 3 feet/1m high
Aspect:	Sun

A rhubarb plant will be productive for up to 15 to 20 years and is winter hardy, growing from crowns which will regenerate regularly, allowing you to grow more and more plants. Once the plant has finished producing stems, the crown lays dormant in winter and can be lifted, divided and replanted, just leave them alone the next year to establish themselves before you harvest any stems. Newly planted rhubarb should not be harvested in the first year to allow the plant to fully establish itself.

The shoots start to appear in mid to late spring as tiny leaves bunched up on a small stem which then grows into the long stems which you harvest when they are between two and three feet long. Pull the stem from the bottom and it should pull out easily. Cut the leaf from the stem immediately otherwise the stem will go limp. The leaves can be used as a mulch around your gooseberry bushes to prevent pests or put on your compost heap.

 Rhubarb is tolerant of most types of soil, though prefers rich, fertile soils that are well drained. If you are starting a rhubarb patch, then dig in plenty of well-rotted manure or compost first and remember, when siting the plants, it is a permanent bed. Once the plants are in the ground you will only be able to top dress the soil so get plenty of organic material in now.

Rhubarb crowns are planted in early spring about 3 to 4 feet apart and watered in well. Make sure they do not get crowded out by weeds as they can compete for nutrients and sunlight which will hamper the rhubarb's growth.

You can buy rhubarb cultivars that can be harvested at different times of the year and if you are planting more than one crown, then it is worth having different varieties so that you have a longer cropping season. Typically, you finish harvesting rhubarb in mid to late July then leave the rest of the stalks on the plant, so it has the energy to survive the winter. However, if the plant is mature, you can still take some stalks through to as late as early September, though these later harvests can sometimes be bitter and tough depending on weather conditions.

You can force rhubarb by placing an upside-down plant pot over the crown as the first shoots appear. So long as your pot has a hole in the bottom the crowns will shoot up towards the light. This makes very sweet and delicate flavoured stems, but you need to allow the rhubarb to rest the following year, meaning no harvest. If you have multiple rhubarb plants then you can force one crown each year, rotating between them so you get some rhubarb early in the season. It is a prolific plant and you will get a lot of stems from it.

Remember that in the first year after planting, or the first year after moving a rhubarb plant, you do not harvest any of the stalks. Never eat the leaves as they are poisonous, but they make for good compost. Sometimes the rhubarb will send up a flower head which needs to be removed when it appears as the plant will put its energy into the flower instead of the stems.

 Rhubarb is a great plant to grow and is particularly easy to manage. It can be left alone and will produce a bountiful crop year after year, with the minimal interaction from you! Every few years it will benefit from being divided, and every winter you mulch the rhubarb. Apart from that, there's very little else that needs doing with this plant. It is a very popular fruit in England, though less commonly used elsewhere. For its delicious, unusual flavour it is well worth growing at home.

Common Pests and Problems

Rhubarb is a pretty hardy plant and doesn't have a lot of things that bother it. It is favoured by gardeners as it just happily grows in a corner needing very little attention. Diseases are rare and if you see any unhealthy looking leaves, then just remove them and dispose of them.

Slugs and Snails: These are probably your biggest problem, though they cause very little damage to the stems, usually preferring to dine on the leaves. They are only a problem if they start chewing on the crowns before they have grown properly. These pests will hide under the leaves and in the middle of the crown, so you need to pick them off and destroy them. Beer traps and other preventative measures can help, though removing them by hand is by far the most effective way of getting rid of them. Removing any dying or fallen stems will help control the slug population by removing their habitat.

Crown Rot: The crowns can rot if they get waterlogged but so long as you plant them in a free draining soil then this shouldn't be a problem. Avoid covering the crowns when you mulch them, particularly if you are using fresh manure as it will burn them. In cold areas or with a late frost, you can cover the crowns with well-rotted compost.

Harvesting and Storing

The first year you plant rhubarb or the first year after moving a clump of rhubarb, you should not harvest any stalks to allow the plant to establish itself. In the second year, just take a few stalks from each plant and then from the third year, once the plant is fully established, you can harvest as much rhubarb as you want. To avoid damaging the plant, take no more than half the stalks from a single plant.

The best stems to harvest are those that are between 12 and 18 inches long and have a lot of red on them. Grab the stalk towards the base and pull it away from the crown, twisting it slightly. If you prefer, you can use a sharp knife to cut the stem. Remove the leaf immediately after harvesting.

In early to mid-spring, the stems have the most flavour. Those harvested later in the year tend to be stringier, making them better suited for jams, jellies, sauces or stewing.

As the stems start to get thinner and shorter you need to stop harvesting rhubarb. At this time, the plants are storing energy ready for the following year. Mature plants will usually allow you to harvest from them for between eight and ten weeks. A well-established rhubarb bed will keep you, your family and most your neighbours in rhubarb each season!

Rhubarb is best used immediately after harvesting, but it can be processed and frozen. The freshly cut stems will store for about a week in your refrigerator, though will become less crisp over time. You can make them crisper by standing the stems in water before use, though they do lose a little of their flavour. Stems can be chopped and frozen or stewed and frozen, depending on what you plan to use them for.

Recommended Varieties

There are lots of different rhubarb cultivars available. Stores will usually only carry one or two varieties, so you will need to look online at specialist plant suppliers for many of the more unusual and best quality varieties. As rhubarb is quite expensive to buy in the shops, this plant offers great value for money.

Here are some popular rhubarb cultivars:

- Champagne – a good variety for forcing, producing long, thin stalks early in the season.
- Fulton's Strawberry Surprise – produces nice, red stalks that taste great, even later in the season. This cultivar is suitable for growing in large containers.
- Grandad's Favourite – a very early, vigorous cultivar that produces thick stems.
- Timperley Early – a heavy cropper that forces well, susceptible to frost damage. Does not hold its colour well and not the most flavoursome variety.
- Victoria – a late variety with very thick, red stalks tinged with green. An old variety that is popular with gardeners.

Strawberries & Pineberries

Strawberries, *Fragaria ananassa*, are a big favourite with almost everyone and the first strawberry of the year is a sign that summer is here and all of us gardeners look forward to our strawberry crop. You might like strawberries from the store but let me tell you that one you've grown at home is completely different and divine in nature! My little girl will spend hours eating strawberries from the allotment, but bring them home from the supermarket and she won't touch them because they "taste funny", particularly when they are not locally grown!

Most stores stock a variety called Elsanta which stores well and is less prone to damage. While this is a good commercial variety, it is not so good for the buyer because they are lacking in taste compared to other varieties. Growing your own allows you to grow some varieties that have a much better flavour, plus you pick them when they are fresh and tastier. Store bought strawberries are often picked just before they are ripe and fully sweet, so they can survive the journey to the supermarkets.

At a Glance Facts

Planting Time:	February to March or September to October
Flowering Time:	Late spring / early summer
Harvest Time:	June to September, depending on cultivar
Pruning Time:	Remove unwanted runners and leaves in autumn
Hardiness:	Full, though flowers can be damaged by late frosts
Height/Spread:	Small, depending on cultivar
Aspect:	Sunny, though will tolerate partial shade

Strawberries are versatile plants and will grow in full sun or partial shade, though they prefer a well-drained soil. Typically, you buy the plants from a store and then plant them in the spring or early autumn. If you are planting them in spring just pinch off any flower buds so they concentrate on establishing themselves and produce a good crop the following year. Autumn grown plants usually crop the next year.

The plants need to be about one foot apart from each other in rows three feet apart so that they have plenty of room to grow and for you to get between them. Strawberries are shallow rooted plants and work well in planters and containers. In poor soils, grow strawberries in raised beds so they can get the drainage and nutrients they need. Water the plants well, particularly when they are establishing themselves and setting fruit.

 They benefit from a good mulch of well-rotted manure or straw to keep in the moisture and prevent weeds. Some gardeners will plant through thick black polythene for the same effect.

When the fruit starts to form you can put some straw underneath it to keep the fruit off the ground to help prevent slugs and snails causing damage. Birds also like strawberries so you will need to net them before the fruit starts to ripen.

When the strawberries have finished cropping, cut the rest of the foliage down to around 4" above the crown which will allow leaves to grow. Clear away and destroy any leaf debris from around the plants to prevent the build-up of disease and pests. Water well, mulch and leave them over winter for a great crop next year!

After the plants have finished fruiting they will send out runners which can grow to several feet long. Along these runners there will be small plants growing. Underneath each of these plants, put a pot filled with compost and just pin the runner into the soil. Once it has established roots you can cut the runner and move the pot. Alternatively, just cut the runners off if you don't want any new plants. Most people will replace their strawberry plants every three to five years as opinion is that the quality of fruit reduces after this time. Runners are a great source of fresh plants for your garden, so are worth keeping when you are planning to replace or expand your strawberry bed.

Pineberries are a variety of strawberry which have a delicate white fruit that takes on a slightly pink blush when they are ripe. They are prolific growers and need the runners removed to produce fruit. The fruits have a strawberry flavour with a hint of pineapple to them and are absolutely delicious! They are rarer than strawberries but are certainly worth growing for a bit of variety.

Common Pests and Diseases

Strawberries suffer from a few problems, though most of these can be avoided by keeping leaf debris away from the plants, appropriate spacing, and mulching them well.

Slugs and Snails: These are likely to be your biggest problem. Removing debris and other hiding places from around your strawberries will keep these down. Lift the fruit off the ground with straw or grow in containers and regularly check the plants for slugs and snails and remove them.

Birds: A huge problem for strawberries which can be combatted with bird scarers or netting. Net your plants before the fruit is ripe as the birds don't usually wait until the strawberries are ripe before decimating your crop!

Spider Mites: These can slow the growth of strawberries and cause the plant to die. Check for thin webbing on the leaves which turns brown or yellow and use an appropriate spray.

Strawberry Root Weevil: This pest will eat the roots causing the plant to wilt and eventually die. Nematodes will help if you have this pest, but you will need to dig up the area and remove your strawberry plants. Grow a new batch of plants somewhere else to ensure the bug isn't in the soil.

Red Stele Root Rot: Also known as red core this is a serious problem for strawberries, particularly when planted in heavy clay soils or areas with moist soil conditions. The plants will start to wilt and die off from the bottom up and the plants will be stunted with a metallic blue/green discoloration on the young leaves. Older leaves will turn red or yellow and come the heat of summer, the plants will quickly wilt and die. This fungus lives for 15-17 years in the soil, so you need to remove your strawberry plants, destroy them (to be sure you don't transfer the fungus) and replant in another location with fresh plants. There are fungicides available, but these are not recommended for preventative use.

Leather Rot: Another fungal disease which attacks the berries, rotting them when they come into contact with the soil (another reason to lift the berries off the ground). This can develop into crown rot which will kill your plants. There are fungicides you can use if necessary.

Strawberry Leaf Blight: This is a common disease in strawberries and causes rot at the stem end of the fruits. This fungus lives in plant debris on the ground, so you need to make sure you keep your strawberry patch clear of leaves and other plant debris. You can plant resistant varieties of strawberries such as Quebec, Oka and Chambly which will help, though there are sprays available.

Grey Mould: Another fungal infection that you will see as the fruit and leaves turn grey with mould. It spreads through the air, water or even when harvesting your strawberries. Make sure you have sufficient spacing between your plants and that you remove all leaf debris from the ground. You need to ensure there is enough air flow around the plants. Put a mulch down to prevent spores splashing up from the ground and water early in the morning so the plants have more time to dry out. There are fungicides available that will treat this if required.

Powdery Mildew: Another fungal disease which appears as a grey/white powder on the underside of leaves. Take the same precautions as for grey mould and water at the base of the plants to prevent this from taking hold. There are commercial sprays available to treat this fungus.

Harvesting and Storing

Ripe fruits turn a deep red colour all over and are slightly soft. All you do is carefully pick them off the plant and then enjoy them! If you are lucky then some of them will actually make it in to the kitchen! Put your harvest in shallow containers as strawberries are delicate and will easily get damaged if you try and stack them deeply in a bowl.

Strawberries will keep for several days in your refrigerator and do not freeze well. They are good dehydrated and make a superb jam or jelly. I would recommend that you make your strawberry harvest into something before you freeze it or just enjoy the fresh strawberries!

Recommended Varieties

There are many different types of strawberry plant available, though there are two main varieties, perpetual and summer fruiting. The former will fruit throughout the growing season whereas the latter have a specific time they produce fruit. Different cultivars will produce fruit at different times during the season. I recommend that you have several different varieties so that you have strawberries throughout the fruiting season rather than a glut.

Here are some of popular strawberry cultivars:

- Cambridge Favourite – a popular variety that has few issues with disease yet is very tasty
- Alice – a mid-season fruiter with great disease resistance and a sweet flavour
- Elsanta – a popular commercial variety that produces plenty of large, tasty fruits, though it can be prone to diseases
- Hapil – a mid-season, heavy cropping variety producing very sweet fruit
- Honeoye – an early cropper with a good taste, though is susceptible to mildew
- Florence – a late season variety with good disease resistance and taste
- Mara de Bois – a perpetual variety that produces fruits with an intense flavour similar to wild strawberries

How to Dry Fruit

Drying fruit is another great way to preserve your fruit and can be used as a snack by themselves, eaten as a trail mix with nuts, used in cooking or served with yogurt or porridge.

While you can buy dried fruit from the stores, this is usually treated with a chemical such as sulphur to preserve it. Your home-made dried fruit will be completely chemical free, meaning you know it is really good for you!

Sometimes dried fruit will lose some of its colour during the drying process. If you pre-treat your fruit by dipping it in lemon or pineapple juice it will help to preserve the colour and reduce browning, particularly in fruits such as apples and pears.

For fruits such as apricots and plums that have stones in them, you can pre-treat them very easily which will help them to retain their colour plus have a light glaze to them. Simple dissolve one-part honey to two parts water and heat the solution until the honey is completely dissolved. Allow it to cool then add the fruit and leave to soak overnight before removing and drying.

Fruits like grapes and blueberries naturally have a waxy coating which can make drying more difficult.

With these, just pop them in boiling water for two minutes which will make them easier to dry.

There are two main ways for you to dry your fruit, either in an oven or using a dehydrator. If you are going to dry a lot of fruit, then it is worth investing in a dehydrator as it is easier to use and much faster than using your oven.

Oven Drying

This is a good way to dry fruits such as apples. Heat your oven to a low heat, 250F/130C. Wash and slice the fruit finely and then arrange in a single layer on a baking tray. Leave in the oven with the door propped slightly open until dry, which can take several hours. When cooled, store them in an airtight container and eat within three to four weeks.

Using A Dehydrator

There are plenty of dehydrators on the market and you can buy one of a suitable size for your requirements. Some of the larger ones can even be used to dry meat and pasta!

Your dehydrator needs to be positioned in a place with good air flow to prevent the damp air from the fruit being sucked back in to the machine.

Follow the manufacturer's instructions for use, though typically you layer the fruit in a single layer making sure they do not overlap.

Preparing the Fruit

You will need to rinse the fruit and then remove any pips, stems or damaged parts of the fruit. Pat it dry with paper towels before drying it and slice it thinly using a sharp knife. You are aiming for all the pieces to be of a similar size to ensure they dry evenly. Fruit such as pears, citrus and apples can be dried without peeling.

Different fruits take different times to dry based on the thickness of the slices and the moisture content of the fruit. Try to always choose ripe, firm fruits that are freshly picked as the sugar content and therefore taste will be higher. Cutting the fruit into evenly sized slices or chunks helps to make sure it all dries at the same time.

The End Product

Your dried fruit will be leathery and pliable without any damp spots. Leave the fruit to cool then tear a piece in half. If it is still moist when you squeeze it then it needs to dry for a bit longer.

Your dried fruit can be stored in a cool, dark place in sterilized jars or paper bags and will store for about a month.

You can rehydrate your fruit for use in cooking or to eat by putting it in a cup of boiling water and letting it stand for about half an hour before use.

Drying fruit is a great way to deal with a glut of fruit and to preserve some of your fruit for several weeks. It makes for a great, healthy snack and is useful in your cooking too!

How to Freeze Fruit

Another popular way of preserving fruit is to freeze it. It's a quick alternative to bottling or drying and is very convenient for many of us. It also keeps more of the nutrients in the fruit, which can be stored for up to a year if properly packed before freezing. However, not all fruits are suitable for freezing without processing in some way first.

Like other forms of preserving you need firm fruit that is just ripe. Any fruit which is overripe can either be eaten or used in cooking over the next few days. Rinse and blanch your fruits before you freeze them and freeze them as quickly as you can after harvesting them to preserve their flavour. Avoid any damaged or bruised fruits.

If you lay the fruit out on to baking trays, making sure they aren't touching, they will freeze individually. The frozen fruit can then be bagged up and when you come to use it they are not all frozen together so you can use as much or as little as you need without having to defrost the whole bag of fruit. Most of us though will just use zip lock bags and freeze portion sized bags of fruit ... it's much quicker and more convenient!

Berries, currants and smaller fruits can all be frozen whole though bigger fruits will need peeling, coring, the pips removed and chopping before they can be frozen. For fruits that go brown when cut, like apples, soak them in lemon juice for an hour or two before freezing to preserve their colour.

Most fruits are not suitable for eating raw when they have been defrosted because they are made up of a lot of water. The texture and consistency changes after defrosting. This is caused by water crystalizing within the cells and damaging the cell walls. When it is defrosted the fruit will be much softer.

Cooking or blanching the fruit first will help minimize this damage as will rapid freezing. The longer it takes the fruit to freeze, the more damage is caused to the cellular structure. This is one reason people spread their fruit out on baking trays because the smaller pieces of fruit freeze quicker than a big bag of fruit so there is less damage.

Another problem you can encounter is freezer burn, which is when moisture is lost from fruit inside the freezer, creating brown spots in the fruit which becomes dry and tough. Put your fruit in heavy duty freezer bags or other plastic containers and make sure that they are air tight. This should prevent freezer burn from happening. I would strongly recommend a vacuum sealer to prevent freezer burn. These store your fruit in high quality plastic bags and then remove all the air before sealing the bag. The result is vacuum packed fruit that will last for two or even three years in your freezer with no discoloration.

Most fruits will freeze and remain usable for between eight to twelve months though you can make them last longer by blanching them in a sugar syrup before freezing.

Raspberries, rhubarb, gooseberries, blackberries, cranberries, blueberries and blanched apples will all freeze really well. Most other fruits can be stored in a sugar syrup solution which is made by dissolving 24oz/675g of sugar into 2½ pints/ 1½ litres of water.

The best way to defrost your frozen fruit is to leave it in the freezer container at room temperature until defrosted. Put the container in some warm water to defrost it faster, but you should ideally eat the fruit cold and when it is defrosted.

One of my favourite recipes for frozen berries is to put about ½ pound of them still frozen in to my blender together with three tablespoons of sweetener (adjust to taste), 8oz/250ml vanilla yogurt and a teaspoon of vanilla extract. Whizz it up and it makes a delicious ice cream.

Your frozen fruits will keep you going through the winter and are great for using in crumbles or other recipes.

Endnote

With the rising cost of living, more and more people are turning to growing their own produce at home in order to save money. With experts recommending that more fruit and vegetables are eaten for the many health benefits they confer on you, it can be expensive to try and ensure you get your five portions per day.

Growing your own fruit at home is a great way for you to get healthy, delicious fruit for pennies on the pound! Why spend a few pounds for a pound of apples when for a little bit more you can buy a tree that will provide you hundreds and hundreds of apples for years to come?

For anyone who is concerned about the environment, growing your own fruit makes sense because store bought fruit is often transported across hundreds or even thousands of miles. This mileage has a major effect on pollution and you can limit your carbon footprint by growing your own fruit at home.

However, not everyone will be able to grow all types of fruits. Some fruits prefer hotter climates and those of us in more northerly areas will have to still buy it from the store or invest in heated greenhouses or sunrooms, which adds to both the cost and environmental impact.

However, wherever you live there are fruits that you can grow natively, outside, with the minimum of effort. Remember that Mother Nature has been growing these fruits for eons without human help, so she knows what she is doing! These things grow like crazy and produce tons of fruit. With a helping human hand though you can minimize diseases, increase yield and ensure your tree remains healthy for many years to come. If you do live in a more northerly area, look at the fruits that grow natively where you are and grow varieties of those, or look for cold hardy cultivars of other fruits.

Having grown a variety of my own fruit at home for many years now I can strongly recommend that you do so. There is nothing like the taste of home grown produce; it is fresh and tastes so much more 'real'.

Growing your own fruit is fun for your children as well. They will love going out and picking the fresh fruit and eating it, plus you will find it is a great way to encourage them to eat a healthier diet.

Gardening is also excellent exercise for you and studies have shown that people who garden are typically fitter and weigh significantly less than those who do not. It gets you outside, gets you moving, and keeps the mind active too; all of which have significant health benefits for you.

Start by selecting which fruits you can grow in your area and then get some plants – you can find these in local stores or order them from the Internet. Remember that fruits are seasonal, so you will tend to only find them in the stores at planting time and most websites will only send them to you at this time too.

You cannot hurry fruits, but if you look after the plants well, they will produce an abundant crop of fruit for you. It doesn't take a lot of work to look after your plants, but you will be pleased with the results when you do.

Growing your own fruit should be a must for most people, whether you grow some strawberries in hanging baskets, dwarf or patio varieties of fruit trees or plant and orchard is up to you, your budget and the space available. Having delicious, fresh fruit to hand is a real benefit and will help save you money and improve your health.

About the Author

 Jason has been a keen gardener for over twenty years, having taken on numerous weed infested patches and turned them into productive vegetable gardens.

One of his first gardening experiences was digging over a 400 square foot garden in its entirety and turning it into a vegetable garden, much to the delight of his neighbours who all got free vegetables! It was through this experience that he discovered his love of gardening and started to learn more and more about the subject.

His first encounter with a greenhouse resulted in a tomato infested greenhouse, but he soon learnt how to make the most of a greenhouse and now grows a wide variety of plants from grapes to squashes to tomatoes and more. Of course, his wife is delighted with his greenhouse as it means the windowsills in the house are no longer filled with seed trays every spring.

He is passionate about helping people learn to grow their own fresh produce and enjoy the many benefits that come with it, from the exercise of gardening to the nutrition of freshly picked produce.

He often says that when you've tasted a freshly picked tomato you'll never want to buy another one from a store again!

Follow Jason and watch his gardening and allotment videos at www.YouTube.com/OwningAnAllotment for a video diary and tips. Join him on Facebook for regular updates and discussions at www.Facebook.com/OwningAnAllotment.

Follow Jason on Twitter and Instagram as @allotmentowner for regular updates, news, pictures and answers to your gardening questions.

Jason has published numerous gardening books, all of which are available on Amazon on Kindle and in paperback, through www.GardeningWithJason.com including:

- Canning and Preserving at Home – A Complete Guide to Canning, Preserving and Storing Your Produce
- Companion Planting Secrets – Organic Gardening to Deter Pests and Increase Yield
- Cooking With Zucchini - Delicious Recipes, Preserves and More With Courgettes: How To Deal With A Glut Of Zucchini And Love It!
- Greenhouse Gardening - A Beginners Guide to Growing Fruit and Vegetables All Year Round
- Growing Chillies – A Beginners Guide to Growing, Using & Surviving Chillies

- Growing Garlic – A Complete Guide to Growing, Harvesting & Using Garlic
- Growing Giant Pumpkins – How to Grow Massive Pumpkins At Home
- Growing Tomatoes: Your Guide to Growing Delicious Tomatoes At Home
- Growing Herbs - A Beginners Guide To Growing, Using, Harvesting and Storing Herbs
- How to Grow Potatoes - The Guide To Choosing, Planting and Growing in Containers Or the Ground
- Indoor Gardening for Beginners: The Complete Guide to Growing Herbs, Flowers, Vegetables and Fruits in Your House
- Keeping Chickens for Beginners – Keeping Backyard Chickens from Coops to Feeding to Care and More
- Raised Bed Gardening – A Guide to Growing Vegetables In Raised Beds
- Save Our Bees - Your Guide To Creating A Bee Friendly Environment
- Worm Farming – Creating Compost at Home with Vermiculture

Jason also loves to grow giant and unusual vegetables and is still planning on breaking the 400lb barrier with a giant pumpkin. He hopes that with his new allotment plot he'll be able to grow even more exciting vegetables to share with his readers.